A SHORT HISTORY OF
FARMING IN BRITAIN

7

1 Interior of Tithe Barn, Harmondsworth, Middlesex.

A SHORT
HISTORY
OF
FARMING
IN BRITAIN

by

Ralph Whitlock

Republished by
EP Publishing Limited
1977

First published 1965 by John Baker, London

Republished 1977 by
EP Publishing Limited
East Ardsley, Wakefield
West Yorkshire, England

ISBN 0 7158 1208 4

Please address all enquiries to EP Publishing Limited
(address as above)

Printed in Great Britain by
The Scolar Press Limited
Ilkley, West Yorkshire

CONTENTS

CONTENTS

ILLUSTRATIONS

ILLUSTRATIONS

9

1

SUBSISTENCE FARMING

The indigenous cattle of Britain – Origins of British breeds of cattle – Origins of sheep – Origins of pigs – Origins of horses – Origins of poultry – Early dogs and cats – Cereals – Cultivations – Other agricultural arts – Early villages on the chalk – The modernity of Roman farming – The coming of the Saxons – Saxon crop rotation – The village waste – Common rights – A Saxon manor

THE foundations of farming were established in prehistory. Nearly all of our farm animals and most of our basic tools of cultivation and husbandry were introduced long before written records.

Palaeolithic and Mesolithic men were primarily hunters, and stock-rearing was apparently introduced to Britain by Neolithic invaders who began to arrive about 2500 B.C. They had cattle, sheep and pigs. As these animals had been domesticated at least three thousand years earlier in Iraq the science of stock-breeding obviously did not originate here. Whether the newcomers brought their livestock with them or whether they applied the techniques of domestication to the wild beasts they found here is not known.

THE INDIGENOUS CATTLE OF BRITAIN

At least two species of wild cattle seem to have been indigenous to Britain. They are the aurochs, or *Bos primigenius*, and the 'Celtic' shorthorn, or *Bos longifrons*, and of them experts now agree that the aurochs was the first to be tamed by man. Perhaps 'tamed' is too definite a word, for the first aurochs may well have been exploited in great, semi-wild herds, as on ranches in the newer countries of the world. Anyhow, the remains of *Bos primigenius* are associated, apparently domestically, with human remains several centuries before *Bos longifrons* puts in an appearance, according to present knowledge.

This, incidentally, seems rather surprising, for the aurochs was a truly formidable beast. The bulls were black, with a brown line down the back, huge, powerful and equipped with horns which sometimes had a span of over three feet. A remarkable scientific achievement of recent years has been the breeding-back, by Dr Heinz Heck of Munich, of the aurochs from domesticated breeds of cattle. Using a mass of material from most of the primitive breeds of Europe, including our Highland cattle, Dr Heck succeeded in re-creating a species which became extinct in 1627. His herd breeds true and is identical with the ancient aurochs, to judge from surviving pictures and descriptions. Moreover, it possesses two notable characteristics. Although bred from domesticated animals, these new aurochs are wild and fierce, and they have also a remarkable resistance to foot-and-mouth disease.

Domestication seems, in the course of centuries, to have reduced the size of *Bos primigenius*, probably through a natural tendency of primitive men to kill the biggest animals for meat and breed from the survivors.

Bos longifrons was a smaller and more delicately built species, reminiscent of a Jersey or Kerry cow. In the Bronze Age it seems to have replaced *Bos primigenius* as the most popular type of cattle.

Origins of British Breeds of Cattle

To trace existing breeds back to these earliest beginnings is extremely difficult, but we may speculate on their likely origins. *Bos primigenius* is almost certainly the chief ancestor of the Highland and Longhorn breeds. From *Bos longifrons* are probably derived the Shorthorns, Channel Island breeds, Kerries and Old Gloucester. There existed from very early times (the earliest so far known being an unmistakable example from an Early Iron Age village at All Cannings, Wiltshire) a polled strain of cattle of unknown origin. It was probably the ancestor of the present polled breeds, or at least some of them, including the Aberdeen-Angus, Galloway and British White. This last is a very ancient breed which has a very similar counterpart in the native cattle of northern Sweden. It is interesting to note, too, that in parts of North Wales a definitely polled strain of the Welsh Black exists.

Cattle were probably brought over by the Danes and, earlier, by the Anglo-Saxons, and these imports may have been one of the origins of our red breeds, notably the Red Polls, Sussex, Devons and Herefords. The last-named, however, probably derive from a cross with a native breed, as the white stripe along the back and tail, which is duplicated in the Old Gloucester breed, indicates.

Finally, there is the tradition that white cattle were introduced by the Romans. The Chillingham herd of wild white cattle are said by some authorities, though their thesis is by no means accepted by all, to have descended from such an imported herd. While this is possible, the theory is unnecessary to explain the facts. The Chillingham cattle could well have evolved from one of the indigenous types and indeed show, apart from their colour, affinities with the primitive Welsh Black.

The Friesian, of course, is a very recent importation from the Netherlands, while the South Devon has both Channel Island and Devon blood in it, with, I suspect, a possible infusion of Charolais.

Origins of Sheep

Sheep are not indigenous to Britain, but were introduced by Neolithic man. The most primitive type is the still surviving

Soay sheep, feral on the island of Soay in the St Kilda group, which seems to be based on two wild breeds, the mouflon of central Europe and the urial of the Near East. All British breeds have a similar mixed ancestry.

It is probable that milk was the primary reason for the domestication of the sheep, with wool as a by-product. Whole sheep-skins had an early economic importance, and the tallow was valuable. The keeping of sheep for meat seems to have been a later development. In passing, it is interesting to note that the primitive Soay sheep yields its wool to plucking; it does not have to be shorn.

Archaeology finds it difficult, often impossible, to distinguish between the bones of sheep and goats. Although goats have ceased to play an important part in the general farm economy, they had their value, chiefly as milk-producers, in subsistence agriculture. Originating in the eastern Mediterranean, they probably came to Britain with the earliest importations of sheep.

ORIGINS OF PIGS

There is a similar archaeological difficulty in differentiating between wild and domesticated pigs. Pig bones are abundant at Neolithic sites, but whether they belonged to domesticated swine or to genuinely wild ones is controversial. Maybe the two phases were interchangeable, captured wild piglets being taken to the farmstead for domestication and domesticated pigs escaping to the forest. Until about two hundred years ago few attempts were made to improve the quality of pigs, which remained razor-backed scavengers in woods and on dung-heaps for at least two millennia. In Britain improvement began with the importation, between 1770 and 1780, of Chinese pigs. It seems, however, that similar pigs from China, based on the sub-species *Sus scrofa vittatus* from south-east Asia, found their way to the Mediterranean in the days of the Roman Empire and there laid

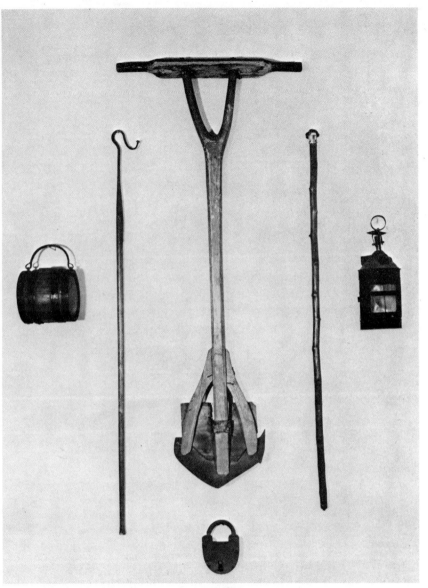

2 A breast-plough; shepherd's crook; shepherd's staff; plough bottle for carrying beer or cider; horn lantern; padlock.

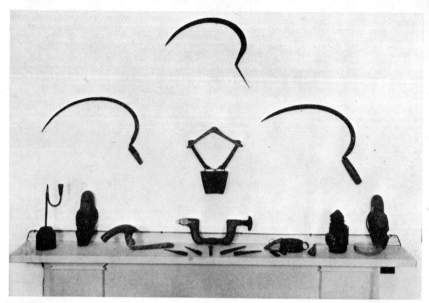

3 Sickles; eighteenth-century brace with set of bits; pair of patterns;
Gloucestershire sheep bell; rush-light holder; eighteenth-century
trowel; and a tinder-box. Collection of Bernard Miles, Esq., London.

4 Long plough from Tewkesbury Vale; a pit saw; wheelwright's tools.

the foundation of several breeds, such as the Neapolitan, which also contributed to our own stock towards the end of the eighteenth century.

ORIGINS OF HORSES

The horse was an animal indigenous to Britain and was at first a quarry of hunters. Neolithic men, in whose settlements the remains of horses are frequently found, ate it and probably milked it, but did not ride it. By the Late Bronze Age horse harness, such as bits and bridles, are found in tombs, indicating that by this time the horse had been domesticated. The likelihood is that the art of horse-riding began on the steppes of central Asia or south-east Europe and spread from there to Britain.

Experts continue to disagree about the origin of the various breeds of horses. It may be said, however, that an important contribution was made by the tarpan, *Equus przevalskii*, the wild horse of central Europe which became extinct as recently as 1878. The tarpan, incidentally, is another extinct animal resurrected by Dr Heinz Heck by the same genetic wizardry as he employed with the aurochs. In Britain the place of the tarpan seems to have been taken by a small species named *Equus agilis*, the chief ancestor of the Celtic pony. Remains of horses prior to the Roman invasion are all of small creatures, many comparable to modern ponies of the Exmoor and New Forest breeds, but some smaller even than the Shetland.

There was also apparently a large, heavy-headed type of indigenous horse in the forests and plains of northern Europe, domesticated by the German tribes but not introduced into Britain till Roman times. The Roman army arrived, of course, with well-equipped cavalry units in which several types of horse, the product of many generations of controlled breeding, were found, and henceforth the blood of all the races of horses in the ancient world went into the British studs.

F.I.B.–B

Origins of Poultry

Domestic poultry originate from several species of jungle-fowl found in India and south-east Asia. They probably spread gradually across the Near East in classical times and may well have been introduced to Britain by the Romans for cock-fighting.

The origin of domestic ducks and geese is lost in antiquity, but both occur wild in this country, and the transition to semi-domesticity is not difficult. The turkey, of course, is a comparative newcomer, being the sole major contribution of the New World to our agricultural livestock.

Early Dogs and Cats

Dogs were perhaps the earliest domestic animals of all, being apparently well established in this country in the Mesolithic era. Remains of dogs are abundant at Neolithic sites. Cats, on the other hand, came late to Britain, perhaps in the ninth or tenth centuries A.D.

Cereals

Wheat and barley were both extensively cultivated by Neolithic men. The original home of wheat grasses, from which the cultivated types derive, seems to have been central and south-western Asia, while that of barley was western Asia and north Africa. Barley was held by the ancient Greeks to be the oldest cultivated plant, and Dr E. S. Beaven considered the beginning of its cultivation might have to be put back to '20,000 or even 50,000 years ago or indeed to an even earlier period'. At Early Iron Age sites in this country both six-rowed and two-rowed ears of barley are found, as well as emmer wheat.

Oats may well have been developed from the indigenous wild oats and were certainly cultivated in Britain early in the Iron Age.

Rye, on the other hand, was a late introduction, probably by the Saxons, from Europe.

A very small bean has been found at certain Iron Age sites.

CULTIVATIONS

As with the origins of our livestock, so the origin of our tools of cultivation is unrecorded. We can speculate that cultivation began with the scratching of plots of soil with a branch or antler in order to provide a better seed-bed. An early development must have been the breast-plough, used in southern England up to little more than a century ago for cultivating steep hillsides and perhaps still occasionally employed on Scottish crofts. This was traditionally used by two persons, often man and wife, one pushing the plough and the other providing extra power by pulling it by a rope. One can imagine the small rectangular plots of the Iron Age, still visible on many hillsides, being cultivated by this implement.

The earliest ploughs did not turn a furrow, but simply scratched the soil. Both mould-boards and wheels were, however, well known in Roman times and may well have been introduced to Britain either then or earlier. Oxen were probably used as draught animals by the pre-Roman Britons, though to what extent is not known. Some Iron Age fields, already mentioned, would seem to be too small for the convenient use of a team of oxen, but we must remember that traces of such early cultivation survive chiefly on land which has since been considered not worth cultivating. All trace of early activities on the better soils will long since have been obliterated. The fact that Roman ox-shoes have been found in Britain indicate that oxen were used on the hard-metalled Roman roads. Although Queen Boadicea's chariots were presumably drawn by horses, it is unlikely that horses were employed on general farm work before Norman times.

From early days mattocks were doubtless used for pulverizing clods, and spikes set in wooden frames were an obvious substitute for a tree-branch for harrowing. Though their development and derivation are obscure, by Roman times nearly all the simple farm implements and tools were in use. Farmers in Romano-British villages used ploughs, spades, prongs, hoes, reap-hooks, scythes, picks and shovels, all differing very little from modern types. The local smith could make not only these commodities but also more elaborate devices, such as padlocks, pumps and scales.

OTHER AGRICULTURAL ARTS

No doubt basketwork, for such purposes as carrying seed-corn, was in more general use than nowadays, and the arts of thatching and weaving with straw probably flourished. For threshing, any one of three methods, namely, treading by oxen, knocking out over a wooden frame, or beating by flails, may have been practised, but the flail is certainly a very ancient implement. Querns, or hand-mills, were probably introduced by the Romans, as were water-mills and perhaps windmills.

Even before the Roman era certain agricultural techniques which we regard as modern were being practised. At Little Woodbury, near Salisbury, careful excavation has thrown light on the economy of a village occupied in the third, second and first centuries B.C. Prominent are the pit siloes in which grain, after threshing and heat-drying, was stored. These siloes, which were probably lined with basketwork, are numerous in many Iron Age sites, one reason being that, owing to a build-up of bacterial infection, each could be used for only a few years.

EARLY VILLAGES ON THE CHALK

The chalk ridges that sweep diagonally across England offered the easiest soils for cultivation by Neolithic men, and it is here that we find the earliest agricultural settlements. In spite of the fact that the southern downs must have been fairly thickly populated, as is implied by the clustering of so many barrows and earthworks around such sacred sites as Stone-henge, and in spite of the series of invasions which must have occurred in prehistoric ages, life on the whole seems to have been peaceful. Many of the early villages were unfortified, apart from stockades to keep out wild animals and occasional raiders, and the oldest circular earthworks which crown the chalk crests were evidently nothing more than cattle corrals. It may be significant that, within living memory, some of the oldest downland sheep fairs were held within the ramparts of hill-top earthworks.

Around the village, extending farther and farther as the population increased, were grouped the village fields. Little Woodbury had 20 acres of them. Most fields are quite small and rectangular in shape, and they may well have been fenced with hawthorn hedges, the laying of hedges being a craft known to have been practised in pre-Roman times. Some of the small, stone-walled fields still to be seen in Wales and Devon may possibly belong to the Bronze Age. Lynchets, or hillside terraces, probably date from the Early Iron Age.

THE MODERNITY OF ROMAN FARMING

In studying the early development of agriculture we are presented with a picture of long centuries of development, doubtless with occasional setbacks but steady on the whole, during which most of the basic discoveries and experiments on which modern farming rests had been made. The Roman era, to which it all leads, is surprisingly modern. We see great estates engaged in producing wheat and wool for export (though wheat had been exported before the visit of Julius Caesar in 55 B.C.). Forests were felled, towns established, and extensive drainage schemes carried out in the Fens and else-where. The Roman period does not, in fact, belong to this chapter. In it farming had ceased to be a subsistence economy; farms were managed to produce surpluses for sale. From the Roman farm to the farm of the early nineteenth century is only a very short step. If the intervening centuries could be missed out, the story of development would read quite naturally. Yet fifteen of those centuries lie between.

THE COMING OF THE SAXONS

Though the Dark Ages still retain their obscurity, it seems fairly certain that, apart from Kent and a few other favoured localities, the face of Britain was pretty thoroughly depopulated before the Anglo-Saxons started to move in. They came up the river valleys and formed their settlements there instead of cultivating the more easily worked but less productive soil of the hill-tops, as the Celts had done.

The Saxon settler ploughed with a team of oxen, four in early times, but later double that number. His heavy plough was cumbersome to turn and so, instead of forming square or rectangular fields, he made them as long as possible. The English measurement of a furlong is, of course, derived from 'furrow-long'.

He was a free man, wresting a living from the soil for his family by his own labour, thus exemplifying the purest form of subsistence farming. The holding he carved out for himself thus tended to be the maximum that one man could cultivate in a year. The settlements were, however, composed of a number of such independent farmers, among whom a good deal of co-operation was essential. For instance, it is unlikely that a single man, especially a new immigrant, would possess enough oxen for a plough team as well as all the implements of cultivation. So they helped each other, each providing what he had and receiving assistance from the others in proportion to his contribution.

From this, in conjunction with the pattern determined by the type of plough, arose the Saxon strip system of fields. A large field adjacent to the settlement would be divided into strips, each of about half an acre, representing a day's plough-ing. The neighbours, pooling their resources, ploughed a strip for each man in turn, then started on the list again. Consequently each farmer had a series of strips scattered about the countryside and, incidentally, thus acquired a fair share of both good and poor soil. These strip-fields, now mostly laid down to permanent pasture, can still be easily traced in many parts of England, notably in the Midlands.

SAXON CROP ROTATION

A consequence of this system was the development of crop rotation. We can imagine farmers discovering that it is possible to overcrop soil. When yields started to diminish the natural course was to leave the field and break up virgin soil elsewhere. After a few years it might be safe to go back and try the first field again. As permanent settlements multiplied and the population increased, so the supply of land was found to be limited and a regular sequence of cropping was introduced.

Generally it was a three-course rotation. The arable land around the village was divided into three large fields. In one wheat (an autumn-sown crop) was sown, in the second barley (a spring crop, thus staggering the sowing season), and the third was left vacant. As time went on it was found to be advantageous to cultivate the fallow during its year of idleness. This open-field system is still practised in the parish of Laxton, in Nottinghamshire.

THE VILLAGE WASTE

Beyond the arable fields lay the 'waste', which could be fen, forest, downland or mountain, where the cattle and sheep grazed. There was also in most parishes good grass-bearing land, usually by streams, which was divided among the farmers, as with the arable, but which remained as permanent pasture. This provided the valuable hay crop on which the farm animals subsisted during winter, but as a rule only one cut was taken. After a certain date, generally 1st August, the parish meadow-land was thrown open for general grazing.

Common Rights

Each farmer had his own private garden and paddock, behind the farmhouse, and each had common rights. The common was an area of the 'waste' often extending to the very heart of the settlement. Here every farmer had rights, but strictly regulated according to his holding. Sometimes several separate commons existed, one for cattle, another for sheep, another for young stock, and sometimes one exclusively for geese. There were also turf-cutting and gorse-cutting rights on commons, and in woodlands rights of pannage (for pigs) and of cutting green boughs (valuable enough for cattle food in times of drought).

Such was the pattern of subsistence farming evolved by the Anglo-Saxons. In spite of the upheavals caused by the Danish invasions, it remained consistent and indestructible throughout the era, and the Norman king William the Conqueror's Domesday Book gives us a unique picture of the well-ordered society it created.

A Saxon Manor

Here, for example, is a Domesday entry for a manor at Winterslow, in Wiltshire. The earl referred to is the Earl of Morton.

'The same earl holds Winterslev. Harding held it in the time of King Edward, and it was assessed at six hides and a half. Here are seven carucates. Three hides are in demesne, where are three carucates and six serfs. Six villans and twelve cottagers occupy three carucates. Here is a mill of the rent of five shillings, and three acres of meadow. The pasture is a mile and a half square. It is valued at ten pounds. The Abbess of Ambresberie held in the time of King Edward two hides in this manor.'

The interpretation of some of the terms is doubtful. A hide is generally supposed to mean the amount of land considered adequate for the support of a free family with its dependants.

5 Celtic fields near Woodford in the Avon Valley, south of Salisbury.

6 The Aurochs—primeval type of European cattle which became extinct in the seventeenth century and was recreated by back-breeding.

7   A Norfolk type of plough.

8   Drilling and harrowing near Dereham, Norfolk.

9 Shire horse Windmill Ideal, winner, Decorated Horse Class, Shropshire and West Midlands Show, 1964.

10 Typical heavy farm horse.

11 Blue Grey Dun, Old English Game Fowl. Hackle, saddle and shoulders are dark grey, the body is slate-blue.

At an early date it may have been defined as the amount of land which could be ploughed by one plough in a year. A carucate, or ploughland as it is sometimes translated, may be identical. Both measurements could vary according to local custom. If the manor had three open fields, then one of them would remain unploughed each year, and, although a farmer might have rights there, it might not be reckoned in his ploughland. Assuming therefore that an ox team could plough 80 acres a year, and that these 80 acres were in strips in two open fields, there would presumably be about another 40 in the third open field which was at the moment fallow, making the farmer's actual holding 120 acres. And 120 acres is a rough-and-ready estimate of what a hide (or carucate) might amount to in modern terms.

Land in demesne was held by the lord of the manor and not sublet to tenants, though it was, of course, worked for him by the peasantry. A cottager held a cottage and plot of adjacent land, usually about 5 acres, by virtue of a labour service. A villan (or villein) was a peasant occupier entirely subject to the lord. And there is a third class, lowest of the low, the bordar, who rendered menial service for his hovel, which he held completely at his lord's pleasure.

So, then, let us translate this in terms of our example, Winterslow. The Book gives us a picture of life in two reigns, that of Edward the Confessor and that of William I. In the first there were 6½ hides, representing perhaps 780 acres of ploughland. This could be in three open fields of 260 acres apiece. A Saxon named Harding was lord of the manor, though 240 acres belonged to the Abbess of Amesbury.

Twenty years after William the Conqueror came to the throne (in 1086, the date of Domesday) the picture had changed. Harding and the Abbess had disappeared, and the whole manor was held by the Earl of Morton. It had increased in size by 60 acres, there being now 7 carucates instead of 6½. Three hides, or 360 acres, were cultivated directly for the Earl by six·serfs, or slaves, with no doubt their families.

Three hundred and sixty acres were occupied by six villans and twelve cottagers. What has happened to the seventh hide is not stated. This being an upland manor, there are no riverside pastures, and only three acres are set aside as meadow, that is for mowing. The pasture, or common, is, however, very extensive, being 1½ miles square, or 1,440 acres.

This manor of the Earl of Morton's did not correspond exactly with the present parish of Winterslow, three other manors being recorded for the village, though this was the largest. Assuming a family of four for each of the twenty-four villans, cottagers and serfs mentioned, we have a population of about 100 on the manor, deriving their living from just over 800 acres of cultivated land, with 3 acres of hay-meadow and 1,440 acres of common. There were doubtless rather more than this, for we have not included the lord's household.

The manor had a mill and was evidently more or less self-supporting. The Saxon peasants had lost their freedom, yet each had his rights as well as his duties (though doubtless the latter were the more conspicuous) in a rigidly regulated social system. And in a society based on subsistence farming, with little or no reliance on money, a social order as strict as the feudal system must have indeed been necessary.

The eventual transition to a freer one based on production for profit and on cash transactions was slow and uneven. Subsistence farming lingered in places until very recent times and has not yet been completely forgotten. Some would say that, although supported by strong practical considerations, the tied cottage of the farm worker is a relic of the days when a man held his house by virtue of services rendered. (The principle also applies to No. 10 Downing Street!) Lords of the manor still exist in innumerable English villages, where they occupy manor houses and are regarded by the villagers as natural leaders, although they can now command no seigniorial rights from their neighbours.

2
FARMING FOR PROFIT

British exports in pre-Roman times — Farming under the Romans — The effects of the Black Death — The role of the abbey in farming progress — The growth of the wool trade — The communal sheep flock — Reasons for keeping sheep — The growth of markets and fairs — Mediaeval trade exemplified by Southampton — Early enclosures — Suppression of monasteries — Increase of trade — Beginning of the Industrial Revolution — The impoverished peasant — The peasants' last revolt — Gradual improvement — Two thousand years summarized

THE alternative title I considered for this chapter, Farming for a Surplus, was not quite right. A surplus is too difficult to define. Ever since organized states and social classes have existed tribute has been exacted from the farmer, sometimes to placate foreign conquerors, sometimes to support the home administration. In early days this must have been collected in kind rather than cash, and the goods which the farmer thus reluctantly parted with could be termed surplus. Whether they really were surplus to his needs depended on his standard of living, though we may be sure that this was of little interest to the tax-collectors.

BRITISH EXPORTS IN PRE-ROMAN TIMES

Strabo, the Pontine geographer born in 64 or 63 B.C., classifies the exports of Britain as 'corn, cattle, gold, silver, iron, hides, slaves and clever hunting-dogs'. For a hundred and fifty years before the Roman invasion trade with Europe steadily increased, to the particular advantage of those Celtic tribes whose lands lay nearest the Channel coasts. Cunobelinus, Shakespeare's Cymbeline, the chief of the

Catuvellauni tribe from A.D. 5 to 40, styled himself King of the Britons, and from his Hertfordshire headquarters issued gold coinage on which the chief motif was an ear of wheat. We thus get an early glimpse of something more than a subsistence economy, of an agriculture with surpluses which brought a substantial profit at least to somebody.

FARMING UNDER THE ROMANS

Once the country had settled down after the Roman invasion the Romans for several centuries exploited on a large scale its farming potential. The arable areas already producing corn were augmented by new reclamation schemes, the largest being the draining of the Fens. This was undertaken on a truly magnificent scale, as the dykes which still survive testify. One of them, the Lincolnshire Car Dyke, is more than seventy miles long. The work was evidently carried out mainly by members of the Iceni tribe reduced to servitude after their Queen Boadicea's revolt. Dr I. A. Richmond in his book *Roman Britain* points out that archaeologists have looked in vain for traces in the Fens of any large-scale Roman field system, but that local features are characteristically native. 'The conclusion is inevitable', he writes, 'that the natives, once planted on the spot, were left to work the land in their ancestral fashion, virtually no attempt being made to convert them to Roman agricultural methods.' Remains of canalside granaries, however, indicate that the Roman tax-collector was on the spot. No doubt each community worked on a quota system, and if it failed to raise its quota so much the worse for it. Dr Richmond states that although one-tenth or one-twelfth of the yield was a standard rate of taxation for much of the Roman world, the Cranborne Chase area of Dorset (where resistance to the first invasion had been stubborn) was assessed at nearer three-fifths. The penal exactions on the Iceni in the Fens are not likely to have been less.

Such was the probable pattern of the massive export trade

in grain built up by Britain during the long centuries of Roman occupation. In the more docile parts of the country, the quota was probably collected, as rent or share-cropping, by Roman or Romano-British landowners. Where this happened the system approximates very closely to our own and can indeed be classified as farming for profit.

During the latter part of the Roman period there seems to have been a switch to sheep-farming in suitable areas, notably Cranborne Chase and Salisbury Plain. It is suggested that this was partly due to the chalk downs, through the clearance of scrub, having become more suitable for sheep than for cattle, but also to the growth of a demand for British woollen cloth. A woollen mill is mentioned in a contemporary document, supposedly at Winchester, but many of the later Roman villas combined the functions of agricultural estates and small factories, and wool could well have been one of the materials with which they worked. If so, we have not only another example of farming for profit but a foreshadowing of the mediaeval wool trade on which the commerce of England was finally founded.

The Roman occupation provided Britain with what it had hitherto lacked, an urban population. Although the Roman cities were not large, ranging mostly from 100 to 200 acres, they housed members of all the usual trades and professions, the majority of whom were not part-time farmers. As these citizens were not engaged in producing food for themselves, someone else had to be doing it, which implies a considerable amount of farming for profit through trade in local markets. This feature of agricultural life was not to reappear until the growth of mediaeval towns, many centuries later.

The Effects of the Black Death

The visitation of plague, known as the Black Death, in 1348 and 1349 marked the beginning of the re-emergence of agriculture from a subsistence economy, petrified by the feudal system. At least a third, and possibly a half, of the population having perished, the survivors rebelled against the shackles of an outworn system which, in any event, they were now inadequate to sustain. In place of the serf, bound to the soil and to his lord by inalienable duties, there arose the landless labourer, fugitive from the manor which was now powerless to restrain him, and offering his services for cash to whoever would employ him. Instead of peasants occupying their strip-fields by virtue of service rendered to their lord, there came into being a race of tenant farmers paying a cash rent for their land. Both changes implied the use of money between parties who had formerly found it unnecessary. And money, as we know well enough, can only be obtained by selling something, be it labour, service or produce. The incentive was thus provided for the development of a system of farming for profit.

The Role of the Abbeys in Farming Progress

The means of introduction of such a system had already been established. In the reign of King Stephen the Cistercian order came over from France to found its agricultural monasteries which were to play such an important part in the mediaeval economy. In the broad vales of Yorkshire and elsewhere it farmed huge estates which gradually specialized in sheep. While the long-delayed growth of towns in England was beginning to provide a local market for surplus agricultural produce, on the Continent, notably in Flanders, towns were beginning to specialize in manufactured goods and so to offer a market for raw material. Our earliest overseas trade was thus founded on wool exported to the Flemish weaving towns.

The Growth of the Wool Trade

Within the next few centuries the trade assumed enormous proportions and made England wealthy. In *A History of*

British Livestock Husbandry Robert Trow-Smith records that
in 1297–8 the cash receipts from wool for Leicester Abbey
amounted to £220 3s. 10d., or more than one-third of the
Abbey's total income. Even Canterbury Cathedral priory,
which farmed mainly arable estates, derived in 1322 an income
of £687 from flocks of 13,730 sheep, receipts from wool
alone amounting to £350. The annual crop of wool, com-
ments Mr Trow-Smith, was worth about one-half the value of
the live sheep.

So lucrative was the trade that not only the abbey estates
but observant barons and peasants enlarged their own flocks,
until England teemed with sheep. In 1341 Parliament granted
to Edward III 30,000 sacks of wool. Assuming a fleece of
about 1½ lb. in weight and a content of 364 lb. of wool per
sack, we can see that this levy alone implies a population of
7,280,000 sheep of shearable age, and this must have been but
a fraction of the total. At this date the areas of greatest production were evidently East Anglia, the East Midlands and
the Home Counties, which were not the ones in which the
great abbeys predominated, indicating that the lay estates
were by this time deeply involved in the trade.

THE COMMUNAL SHEEP FLOCK

The system whereby the sheep of a parish grazed com-
munally, under the care of a parish shepherd, lingered long.
Thomas Davis, of Longleat, Warminster, describes it as he
found it in Wiltshire when he reported on the country's farming to the Board of Agriculture in 1811:

'The common sheep-down is open for the common flocks
during the summer and autumn. The unsown or summer-field
is also open until it is ploughed for wheat; after that the sheep
have only the down till the harvest is over. When the corn
fields are clear, the flock has those fields and the down till the
winter obliges the owners to give them hay. Until this period
they are folded on the arable fields in a common fold; but

when they begin to eat hay, every commoner finds his own
fold and his own hay, the common shepherd feeding and fold-
ing the whole. This is the ancient custom of managing the
sheep stock in the district.'

He then explains how contemporary farmers were changing
the old custom by putting their own shepherds in charge of
their flocks and continues:

'In some instances, the water-meadows are common for
sheep stock in the spring, are mown in small known lots in the
summer, and are fed by the common herd of cows in the
autumn. . . . Whilst the water-meadows are open, the sheep
are folded on the barley land, and by the time the water-mead
grass is eaten, and the barley sown, the summer-field
(especially if it be sown with ray-grass) is ready to receive
the sheep, where they generally remain till near shearing-
time, when they go to the down until the stubble-fields are
broken, at which time (perhaps about the middle of Sep-
tember) the rams are usually put to the ewes. The rams are
provided, and the common shepherd is paid, at the joint
expense of the commoners.

'As this state of *commonage*, where there must necessarily
be a great scarcity of winter food, requires a reduction of the
sheep stock before winter, it is customary to sell off the old
ewes and the wether lambs about Michaelmas, and to put out
the ewe lambs to be wintered either on pasture lands or on
turnips, in other parts of the same, or in an adjacent county.
. . . And yet, after this diminution of the flock, the common-
field farmers are not infrequently obliged to buy hay for the
remainder, and to fetch it from a distance of ten or fifteen miles.'

Here we have a picture of sheep-farming in the days before
enclosures, which were then proceeding. Although innovations are discernible, the broad pattern is the same as what it
must have been on the mediaeval manor. Changes are indicated by the references to 'ray-grass' and turnips, which the
mediaeval farmer did not know. Similarly, the water-meadows
were, in the main, an eighteenth-century improvement, and it

12 A travelling sheep-shearing gang in 1880.

13   Jonas Webb (*d.* 1862), a leading breeder of Southdown sheep.

14   Old Cotswold Sheep on whose fleece the wool trade of England was founded.

15 Romney Marsh or Kent Ewe, the breed on which New Zealand's flocks were founded.

16 Wiltshire Horn Ram at 3 years old.

17   Prize Hereford Bull owned by the Earl of Warwick, winner at Smithfield Show, 1846.

18   An Aberdeen Angus steer.

is unlikely that farmers of the Middle Ages augmented their supplies of hay by buying from ten or fifteen miles away. Winter food supplies for livestock must have been even more meagre than those which Thomas Davis declares inadequate, though some sheep were housed in winter and had a small ration of cereals and beans.

REASONS FOR KEEPING SHEEP

An interesting difference in the economy lies in the purposes for which sheep were kept. Thomas Davis postulates: 'The first and principal purpose is undoubtedly the dung of the sheep-fold, and the second is wool. The improvement of the carcass was not heretofore thought a primary object' (though in Davis's day it had become a controversial issue).

On the mediaeval estate wool was indubitably the prime and often the only object. A secondary consideration in some districts was milk, especially for cheese, with meat a bad third. It is unlikely that in the Middle Ages the value of the sheep as an agent for fertilizing the soil was widely appreciated. This emphasis on wool resulted in a striking difference in the composition of the mediaeval flock. As wethers give more wool than ewes, farmers kept as many wethers as possible. And they retained them for as long as they would yield wool economically. Ewes were kept in sufficient numbers for replenishing the flock, an approximately equal number of ewes and wethers being a generally satisfactory arrangement, but in time specialist breeding flocks were founded, allowing other flocks to specialize in the more productive wethers. Such specialization began probably on the large monastic estates, where the flock could be split into two parts, one for breeding and the other for wool-production, but it later spread to the lay manors.

THE GROWTH OF MARKETS AND FAIRS

Once the doors of trade had been thrown open an increasing
F.I.B.–C

volume of traffic passed through them. Although urban weaving was at first concentrated in the towns of the Netherlands and Flanders, it was not long before it brought prosperity to English towns, such as Norwich, Lincoln, Stamford, Oxford, London, Winchester and a host of smaller boroughs. The growing urban population naturally provided an increasing market for surplus food from the countryside and gave a stimulus to the production of such commodities as milk, butter, cheese, poultry and vegetables. A feature of the Middle Ages is the increasing number of charters granted for fairs and markets. Here the representatives of abbots and barons, selling their fat beasts and grain, jostled old market-women laden with baskets of onions and pats of butter. The lanes and tracks often thronged not only with the pilgrims, knights, jesters and all the merry company with which we become familiar in *The Canterbury Tales*, but with flocks of sheep and droves of cattle, as well as with pack-horse trains laden with wool (though much wool was transported by barge down the rivers).

MEDIAEVAL TRADE EXEMPLIFIED BY SOUTHAMPTON

The port books of Southampton present a typical picture of a mediaeval port with a thriving trade. Over a thousand visitors a year are estimated to have entered the port annually in the fifteenth century. Most ships at first came from across the Channel, from Gascony, Flanders and Spain, but the trade with the Mediterranean, notably with Italian cities, came to assume even greater importance. Imports included spices, perfumes, silks, carpets, incense, jewels, alum, wine, currants, sugar, turpentine, satin, velvet, articles of gold and silver, parchment, sulphur, figs, candied orange peel, porcelain, leatherwork, almonds, lemons, pomegranates, soap, dyes, quicksilver, cork, furs, tapestries, household utensils, weavers' tools, fish, furniture, glass and unfamiliar African animals, such as monkeys, parrots and ostriches. The export trade consisted overwhelmingly of wool, much of it raw, but some made into various types of cloth. Quantities of tin and lead also passed through the port, and some manufactured goods, notably of pewter.

Trade was so flourishing that it could pay not only for necessities, such as dyes and alum, but for a surprising range of luxuries. While most of the last category doubtless found their way into the homes of merchants and monarchs, there must also have been a demand from rural lords and even from yeomen.

The prosperity implied was not, however, distributed with any equity, and the changes to a profit-making rural economy brought riches to some but hardship to others. Many manors succumbed, and modern archaeologists enjoy the quest for 'lost mediaeval villages'. Some became depopulated by the Black Death; some were abandoned through sheer poverty, largely owing to the exhaustion of the soil by wasteful farming methods; others were deliberately obliterated to make room for sheep farms.

EARLY ENCLOSURES

Although the flood-tide of enclosures did not occur until the eighteenth century, enclosures had, in fact, been occurring from time immemorial. From time to time they provoked temporary protests, particularly when the peasant was dispossessed to make room for sheep. Unrest was sporadic throughout the reigns of Henry VII and Henry VIII, and the action of the peasants of Jack Kett's rising at Norwich, in 1549, of slaughtering 20,000 sheep was symbolic.

SUPPRESSION OF MONASTERIES

Henry VIII's destruction of the monasteries, although it created much personal distress and greatly increased the number of landless labourers who wandered the countryside, made no great impact on agriculture. More often than not the abbot was simply replaced by a local nobleman or merchant, who maintained the greater part of the estate intact and founded the fortunes of many of the great landed families who farm the same fields to this day. Indeed, in one region of the kingdom the change resulted in the addition of an extensive new province, for the Earls of Bedford, who succeeded the monkish owners of the Fens, set about reclaiming that waste of marsh and water which had produced little but eels and waterfowl since Roman times.

Increase of Trade

Not only did the towns increase steadily in size (the population of London rose from about 100,000 in Queen Mary's time to about 200,000 by the end of the reign of her successor, Elizabeth I), but export trade grew in other agricultural commodities than wool (which had declined). Corn was exported on a large scale, and traffic in cattle, sheep, poultry and grain between various parts of the country was considerable. In the reign of Queen Anne the construction of new canals increased this internal trade, and much traffic also was seaborne.

Beginning of the Industrial Revolution

The general pattern of life in rural Britain remained unbroken, however, till the second half of the eighteenth century. It was then that the manufacture of goods began to move in earnest from the cottages of peasants and from the small country towns to new urban conglomerations of the North and Midlands, splitting the ancient economy from top to bottom. The English propensity for trade, fostered slowly throughout the centuries, now burst into exuberance with the exploitation of the juxtaposed deposits of coal and iron in the hitherto undeveloped provinces. Overseas trade, with all corners of the now completely unveiled world, blossomed.

To meet the challenge of feeding the proliferating population of the new towns and also to endeavour to keep pace with the accumulating wealth of city merchants, the descendants of the manorial lords and of the yeomen farmers set about improving their efficiency as food-producers. For them the day of subsistence farming had now irrevocably passed; they were engaged in farming for profit. Unfortunately they shared the villages with a lowly peasant population still largely at the subsistence level, smallholders who eked out a living from a few strips of land, supplemented by meagre rights on the parish common and by craftsmanship.

The Impoverished Peasant

This submerged population was already in trouble. The building of new roads had opened up trade in England. Instead of having to make for their own use everything they needed, villagers could now buy it cheaper (for it was being mass-produced by machinery) in the now-accessible town. The peasant who had formerly, with his family, worked as a weaver, tailor, furniture-maker, brewer or with iron or leather now found the most lucrative part of his livelihood taken away. The other half was about to disappear. The new ideas of crop rotation, providing winter food for livestock in the form of turnips and of hay from clover and rye-grass, and of improving cattle and sheep by intelligent breeding, could not be practised with the common flock, on common lands or in the strip-fields governed by the ancient, rigid, three-course rotation.

The answer of the impatient, progressive and ruthless estate-owners of the period was wholesale enclosure. Between 1760 and 1820 every session of Parliament passed a shoal of enclosure Acts, usually in a completely cavalier manner. The bewildered and dispossessed peasant had the two alternatives of finding employment, if he could, on his rich neighbour's land or migrating to the swollen manufacturing towns.

Severely as it bore on the luckless under-dog, the agricultural revolution succeeded in evolving a pattern of farming able, in some measure, to cope with the problem of feeding the now vast manufacturing population. It did so even during the long period of war with Napoleon, though at soaring prices. Blockade and counter-blockade revealed the fact that Britain had become partially dependent on imported corn from Europe. Corn prices rose to 126s. a quarter, to the great distress of the poor labouring classes, both in towns and in the countryside, though the farmers who had survived the upheaval of the enclosures had never done better.

The Peasants' Last Revolt

The end of the war and consequent sudden collapse of prices brought even greater hardship in the villages, for landowners and farmers, finding their profits dissolving, attempted to correct the situation by cutting labour costs. This they did partly by Parliamentary legislation, notably the passing of the Corn Laws, partly by introducing labour-saving machinery (such as threshing-machines, which occasioned the labourers' despairing revolt of autumn 1830), and partly by reducing wages. The last method was carried to the extreme of making the entire labouring population paupers and subsidizing their wages out of the rates.

Gradual Improvement

Emergence from this morass was slow, but the peace of the Victorian era gave the opportunity for steady and ordered development. Although nothing dramatic had happened, the countryside of the 1860s was vastly more prosperous, at every level, than that of the 1830s. Mechanization was accelerating, production increased, and more and more land was brought under cultivation.

In his *English Social History* Dr G. M. Trevelyan writes:
'But agriculture was not capable of indefinite expansion; by

the middle of the century it had reached its highest development and the acreage of land could not be increased. On the other hand, the Industrial and Commercial Revolution was only then gathering strength, and the increase of town wealth and population went on decade after decade. The Census of 1851 showed that already half the population of the island was urban, a situation that had probably not existed before, in a great country, at any time in the world's history. And, since there was no visible limit to this process, it was ominous of a queer future.'

Two Thousand Years Summarized

Let us pause to summarize the journey we have made so far.

We began with several millennia of subsistence farming, evolved in the earliest days from an economy of hunting and food-gathering. We encountered its first false summer between approximately 100 B.C. and A.D. 400, when Britain became commercially a part of Europe, trading its agricultural surpluses for a wide variety of manufactured and exotic imports.

In the collapse which followed, the long struggle from a purely subsistence level had to begin again. Progress was slow until the twelfth and thirteenth centuries, when the development of the wool trade gave it an impetus. Thereafter it was fairly steady, growing with the growth of towns and of international trade.

The mushrooming of populous industrial towns in the late eighteenth century coincided with the development of agricultural ideas which would make possible the feeding of a rapidly increasing urban population. Putting them into practice, however, necessitated a drastic reorganization of the rural economy, in part aided and in part aggravated by the intervention of the Napoleonic Wars.

The end of the wars increased rural suffering and revealed the faults in the jerry-built edifice. During the next forty or fifty years, through the long, peaceful reign of Victoria, mistakes were slowly repaired and the foundations of a prosperous agriculture more surely laid. By 1870 we see British farming at its zenith and capable, according to Dr Trevelyan, of little further expansion.

And now the situation, says Dr Trevelyan, was 'ominous of a queer future'. If farming, at the limits of production, was just able to feed the contemporary town population, what would happen when, inexorably, that urban population increased?

The answer was largely unforeseen and temporarily ruinous for British agriculture. In 1875 the flood of grain from the newly tapped reservoir of the Middle West of America and Canada began to pour into our ports. It, with the similar imports of meat, has dominated our economy ever since, except when war compels us to look once again to our own fields.

Now the century-old question is being asked again, but this time with the uncomfortable knowledge that, before long, a different answer will have to be found.

3
FOOD FROM OVERSEAS

The destruction of the peasant — The migration to the towns — Cobbett and his visions — Wholesale emigration — The first clash of town v. country — The years of prosperity — How the landowners engineered their own doom — The First World War — The disasters of the 1920s — Recovery begins — The situation in 1939 — The War Agricultural Executive Committees — Farming in 1945 — The 1947 Agriculture Act — The National Agricultural Advisory Service — The European Common Market — The present situation

THE old English open-field system with its fragmented holdings imposed an intolerable impediment in the path of agricultural progress. Enclosures were necessary to provide the framework for the introduction of new crops, the development of a more efficient rotation, the improvement of livestock and all the features of modern farming. We have already noticed, however, how hardly the enclosures bore upon the poor. This was not the only item on the debit side. What happened to farmers and landowners after 1875 might be described historically as a Nemesis for what their ancestors did fifty years earlier.

THE DESTRUCTION OF THE PEASANT

For what the enclosures accomplished was the destruction of the ancient English peasantry. In theory each householder with rights in open field and common was given a plot of land in strict proportion to those rights. There was, however, a large class of rural squatters, many of whose families had been in residence for generations, who had no legal rights and were thus completely dispossessed. Those with establishable rights ranged from the lord of the manor, with perhaps 500 to 1,000 acres, to the cottager with grazing rights for a cow, two pigs and a dozen geese. It could well happen that the lord's share was so large that he could legitimately outvote all the other landholders in the parish, even without the aid of the chicanery characteristic of parliaments of that age. The cottager who had managed to eke out a living by combining seasonal work with the pasturing of his meagre head of livestock on the common now found himself with an acre or so of land incapable of supporting even a small number of animals throughout the year. The situation could be aggravated at will by the lord of the manor, who, in allocating the holdings, could ensure that a difficult neighbour was saddled with his little holding on a barren hillside a mile and a half from home. Moreover, there were the legal expenses to be paid, and many a cottager had to sell his small allotment to his giant neighbour in order to raise the fee. The whole iniquitous story is told in disturbing detail by J. L. and Barbara Hammond in *The Village Labourer*.

What happened to the unwanted peasants?

J. L. and Barbara Hammond show that the enclosure move-ment was at its height between 1761 and 1844. From 1702 to 1762, 246 private enclosure Acts, covering about 400,000 acres, were passed by Parliament. From 1761 to 1801 some two thousand Acts dealt with well over 3,000,000 acres, while from 1802 to 1844 another 2,500,000 acres were covered by just short of two thousand Acts.

The first thing that strikes the student is that the middle of the peak period coincides with the long wars with the French. A lot of surplus manpower must have then been absorbed by the armed forces.

Let us look at some of the other alternatives for the dis-possessed peasant. The obvious recourse was for him to work as a paid labourer on the land of his richer neighbours. This had seemed a desirable release to the serf of the Middle Ages; now it was resented as a bitter necessity. One reason for discontent was that wages were arbitrarily fixed. When in wartime food prices rose attempts were made, notably by Samuel Whitbread, to introduce a statutory minimum wage, linked with the price of bread. The reform was defeated. Instead the notorious Speenhamland system was introduced. This was an alternative worked out by magistrates and others at the Pelican Inn, Speenhamland, Newbury, on 6th May 1795, whereby it was agreed that every labouring man should be entitled to a certain weekly sum, either from his own labour *or out of the parish rates*. The sum, as with the proposed minimum wage, was linked with the price of bread, and provision was made for the worker's wife and family as well as himself. The difference lay in the fact that now the responsibility for providing the money rested not on the employer but on the parish. Its effect was to put, in the next few decades, the greater part of the rural population on parish relief. Moreover, seeing that it provided in effect a family allowance, it gave an incentive to early marriage and large families. From being an independent smallholder the peasant sank to the status of a day labourer, employed at an inadequate wage, burdened with a rapidly increasing family, and forced to go cap in hand for reluctantly given doles.

Nor was there a ready means of escape. The old idea of a link between the man and the land that bred him was still strong and was now reinforced by the Speenhamland settlement. When every labourer was either already or likely to become a liability on the parish, the parish officials vigorously discouraged immigrants from another parish. From the time of Charles II onwards a series of laws of settlement regulated the removal of persons from one parish to another. Summarized, they provided that a man could move if he (*a*) paid parish taxes, (*b*) held a public office in the new parish, (*c*) served an apprenticeship therein, or (*d*) was employed in the parish for a year. Otherwise he was only accepted if he brought with him a certificate from his home parish stating that his home parish would provide for him if ever he became

chargeable on the rates. As the home parish's guarantee
included the responsibility for fetching him back from wherever
he might be, it can be understood that such certificates were
not readily granted. An impoverished labourer could get a
certificate to do seasonal work in the next parish, but not to
make a long journey to try his luck in one of the new manufacturing towns several counties away.

The Migration to the Towns

How, then, did the new manufacturing towns augment their
supply of labour? By accepting labourers without certificates.
When necessary they winked their eye at the law. It was,
however, far easier for a family to get into such a town than to
get out. If officials did not require a certificate, neither were
they disposed to grant one. The result was that, once they
were in, there the immigrants had to stay, accepting whatever
wages and living standards they could get. An influx of newcomers was, in fact, used to provide a reservoir of unemployed
and to keep down the cost of labour.

Such was the dilemma of the dispossessed peasant of the
second half of the eighteenth and first half of the nineteenth
centuries. It was not until after the Napoleonic Wars, when
the sudden collapse of the wartime economy caused even
greater distress, that it began to dawn on the harassed working man that there was another alternative—beyond the
ocean.

Cobbett and His Visions

At first the idea was extremely distasteful to him, but was
fostered by landowners eager to get rid of the 'surplus'
population which now made such heavy demands on the rates.
It was vigorously opposed in the 1820s and 1830s by that
muddle-headed but magnificent English yeoman, William
Cobbett.

Riding down the valley of the Salisbury Avon in August

1826, Cobbett calculated the population which could be fed on the harvest he saw about him. On a fairly liberal standard of living he estimated that the single parish of Milton was producing enough bread for 800 families, enough mutton for 500, and enough bacon and beer for 207, an average of 502 families or, at five to a family, 2,510 persons. Yet he found that the actual population was 500, or about 100 families. He almost burst with indignation.

'So here are about one hundred families to raise food and drink enough, and to raise wool and other things to pay for all other necessities, for five hundred and two families! Aye, and five hundred and two families fed and lodged, too, on my liberal scale. Fed and lodged according to the present scale, this one hundred families raise enough to supply more, and many more, than fifteen hundred families; or seven thousand five hundred persons! And yet those who do the work are half-starved! In the 100 families there are, we will suppose, 80 able working men, and as many boys, sometimes assisted by the women and stout girls. What a handful of people to raise such a quantity of food! . . .'

He goes on to calculate that in the valley of Avon there are '9,116 persons raising food and raiment sufficient for 45,580 persons, fed and lodged according to my scale; and sufficient for 136,740 persons, according to the scale on which the unhappy labourers of this fine valley are now fed and lodged!

'And yet there is an *Emigration Committee* sitting to devise the means of getting rid, not of the idlers, not of the pensioners, not of the deadweight, not of the parsons, not of the soldiers; but to devise means of getting rid of these working people, who are grudged even the miserable morsel they get!'

He castigates unsparingly the philosophy of Malthus, then fashionable, that 'the human kind have a natural tendency to increase beyond the means of sustenance for them'.

It is interesting to try to visualize the England of Cobbett's visions. It has many attractions. Instead of vast conurbations, it is a network of equal-sized towns or large villages, each of two or three thousand souls. Each is fed primarily from its own soil and has its quota of small factories. Apart from the emphasis on home food production, the pattern would resemble that of a modern trading estate with light industries. The worst evils of slums and of the growth of an ignorant population entirely divorced from the healing rhythm of country life could have been avoided. But Cobbett was a lonely prophet saddled with a sentimentality about a past that never was. Indignant over contemporary ills, his remedy was to look back nostalgically to a rural England of a golden age which existed chiefly in his imagination. Such reformers are never wholly effective.

WHOLESALE EMIGRATION

Although many of the earlier emigrants to the new lands overseas were reluctant travellers, being either transported criminals (in the loosest sense of the word) or unwanted paupers, as the nineteenth century proceeded more and more stalwart villagers found in the harsh freedom of Canada, Australia and New Zealand an escape from local tyranny and despair. America also received large quotas of immigrants at a time when the mountains had at last been passed and the plains of the Middle West were offering their vast prospects. It is sometimes forgotten, too, that South Africa attracted boat-loads of farming immigrants from England, especially in the decade 1810 to 1820. New Zealand was settled somewhat later, between 1837 and 1850. The wastelands of Canada were explored and exploited extensively by Highland crofters, fleeing from conditions as harsh as or even more impossible than those prevailing in England, while the Irish potato famines of the late 1840s sent hordes of starving survivors, obsessed with hatred of England, across the Atlantic.

For a generation or two the emigrants pioneered, felling timber, building their log cabins, painfully claiming virgin soil for the plough and rearing large families under austere conditions. By the beginning of the fourth quarter of the nineteenth century the battle was largely won. The new lands were yielding increasing harvests to the plough, the pastures were alive with flocks and herds, the local markets were saturated.

The means now existed to supply distant markets. Railways, replacing the old covered waggons, were beginning to provide rapid transport to the ports, where steamships waited to take cargo across the oceans. Grain, being able to sustain long journeys without special treatment, was naturally one of the first commodities thus to be shipped back to Europe. The flood of grain from the American prairies began in 1875. Ten years later the development of refrigeration opened the way for a similar influx of frozen meat from Australia and New Zealand. The doom of English agriculture was inevitable.

It so happened that the beginning of this Nemesis coincided with a series of unfavourable harvest years in Britain. From 1876 to 1879 the summers were dull and rainy; consequently yields were low and disease rife among cattle and sheep. In the past farmers could expect some sort of compensation, in the shape of rising prices, for this state of affairs. So long as the nation depended largely on its home-grown food supplies, the law of supply and demand ensured this. Now the main sources of supply were beyond reach of the English weather. Far from prices rising to match the bad harvests, they fell, for the only effects of local shortage was to attract more imports. So wheat dropped from 58s. 8d. a quarter in 1873 to 26s. 2d. a quarter in 1896 (the nadir of the depression). Barley fell from 40s. 5d. to 22s. 11d. in the same period, and oats from 25s. 5d. to 14s. 9d. The general price index for farm products was almost halved.

THE FIRST CLASH OF TOWN v. COUNTRY

The situation cast a revealing light on the now deep cleavage between town and country in Britain. Sixty years earlier the two had engaged in a stand-up combat, and rural interests had won. This was when the war with Napoleon had suddenly collapsed in 1815. During that war, with all hope of importing any corn from Europe effectively nullified by the blockade and counter-blockade, prices soared to a pinnacle of 126s. a quarter for wheat in the year 1812. Little was done to relieve the distress of the starving poor in the teeming, ill-organized manufacturing towns. In 1815, however, when prices threatened to tumble dramatically, the Government passed a Corn Law in an endeavour to maintain farming prosperity by restricting imports. Though bitterly opposed by the urban population, from the illiterate mob to the leading city bankers, the Corn Laws dominated English economy till 1846, when, in the face of prophecies of dire calamities, they were repealed. Thereafter the policy was of free trade.

The Years of Prosperity

In spite of forebodings, for the next thirty years agriculture flourished under this policy. Indeed, during those thirty years British farming reached a peak of prosperity hitherto un-known, as, indeed, did the whole nation. Most of the technical developments in agriculture date from that period, as we shall presently see. More land was under cultivation than ever before, even steep hillsides, which only now are being tackled by crawler tractors, being ploughed by breast-ploughs; while new machines, new ideas about manuring, new varieties of plants and improved livestock contributed to the pattern of progress which the Victorians came to regard as inevitable. A more perspicacious generation would have seen that what was inevitable was the downfall of agriculture.

How the Landowners Engineered Their Own Doom

For the landowners who had engineered the enclosure Acts during the previous century or so had done their work too

19 Highland Cattle on Lord Lovat's Estate, Beauly, Inverness-shire.

20 A Longhorn heifer, once a predominant breed of the Midlands.

21   British White Cow, rare breed descended from an original type.

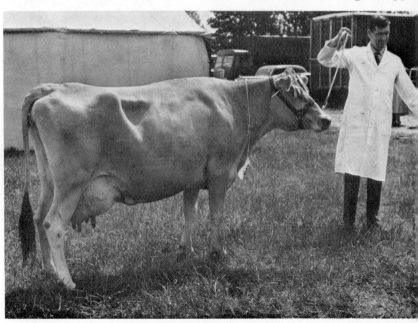

22   Champion Jersey Cow at Three Counties' Show, Malvern.

thoroughly. They had, seeking their own advantage, de-populated the countryside. Vast numbers of former peasants had been driven overseas, where their descendants were now producing a surplus of food which threatened the stability of the home market. Vast numbers of peasants had been driven into the crowded towns, where they had produced a population completely out of sympathy with country life. The emigrants made available the supplies of cheap food; the urban voters ensured that no protective legislation should keep them out.

It was a situation which suited everyone except the farmers, who were by now so whittled down numerically as to be of little account.

The reader will by this time have recognized a familiar situation. We are now almost up to date. The economic pattern which began to develop in the 1870s continued not only for the rest of the century but throughout most of the twentieth—with exceptions. Those exceptions have been times of war. Then the overseas supplies have been cut off by blockade, near-panic has temporarily prevailed, and agriculture has once again become supremely important.

Let us briefly scan the story of these recent decades.

For the twenty years between 1873 and 1893 British agriculture floundered in its depression. The corn acreage declined by some 25%; prices, as we have seen, were nearly halved, and more than 25% of the workers left the land. Rents fell by more than 20%; repairs and rebuilding were neglected; and much farmland relapsed into semi-dereliction. Royal commissions in 1879 and 1893 emphasized the agricultural distress, but did little to alleviate it.

From 1893 onwards a limited improvement occurred. Owing partly to the general increase of population (in other countries as well as Britain), partly to increasing prosperity and hence purchasing power, and partly to wars (in South Africa and elsewhere) which took manpower out of useful production, food surpluses were smaller, and hence prices rose. The improvement was most marked with farm products which made a ready appeal to the new purchasing power of the urban housewife, such as milk, eggs and vegetables. These were commodities in which freshness outweighed price and in which the home producer thus had an advantage. There was, however, a general though less marked increase in price of other farm produce, even of cereals. Britain therefore entered the First World War with an agriculture which was once again becoming moderately prosperous, though far from booming.

The First World War

At first in this war no priority was given to producing food supplies. The situation was too new for this factor to be taken into account, and, in any case, it was expected that the war would be over in a matter of months. As disillusionment set in it was realized that there were other more urgent uses for ships than bringing cargoes of wheat from the other side of the world, besides which the menace of the U-boat lurking beneath the grey Atlantic waters conjured up the unfamiliar and alarming spectre of famine. Once more, as in the Napoleonic Wars, food prices soared. The wheat acreage increased by nearly 1,000,000, oats by 1,100,000, and there was a general increase of farm livestock, except pigs. The place of farm workers shortsightedly conscripted for military service was taken by large numbers of women, and for the first time workers on the land were guaranteed a minimum wage. Towards the end of the war, in 1918, the Corn Production Act was passed to protect arable farmers from the unrestricted overseas competition of the pre-war world. At last the importance of home agriculture seemed to be appreciated by the urban-elected Government.

The Disasters of the 1920s

As soon as the war was over, however, most of the mistakes of the aftermath of the Napoleonic Wars were repeated. This was to be the world of 'no-more-war', in which prosperity and freedom were to increase under the beneficient rule of free trade. Wartime controls were jettisoned as quickly as possible, among them the Corn Production Act, which was axed in 1921; 1924 was the last year of even moderate farming prosperity. By 1925 agriculture had plunged into the depression which, within a few years, was to engulf the whole world in a morass of unexampled misery. That the two events bore any resemblance to cause and effect was unappreciated even by economists. It was not yet understood that the neglect and collapse of a primary industry such as agriculture must inevitably rock the whole edifice of the national economy.

RECOVERY BEGINS

The eventual catastrophe carried within itself the seeds of recovery. Affected even worse than ourselves were the newer countries, notably America. There enormous acreages of land were allowed to go out of production, and the consequent fall in the amount of food available for export had its effect in European markets. The effect of these reduced supplies on our agricultural economy would have been more marked if it had not been for action taken by the new national governments of certain Continental countries, notably Germany and Italy. Seeking to promote the welfare of their own agriculture, in the interests of self-sufficiency against time of war, they raised protective barriers against agricultural imports. The supplies which they might otherwise have absorbed were consequently diverted to other markets, notably Britain.

Although throughout the 1930s imports of foodstuffs by Britain continued to rise, the long reign of free trade drew at last to a close. One of the devices employed by hard-pressed food-producing countries to pay for their essential imports during the depression was to subsidize exports. It gradually dawned upon British Governments that this was the reverse of free trade, presenting as it did an impossible competition to home agriculture.

The Import Duties Act of 1932, therefore, provided the first real step towards protection. Although wheat and meat were excepted, most agricultural imports were thereby protected by an import duty. The measure was only partially successful, from the British farmer's point of view, for it did not apply to produce from the Dominions, and the Ottawa Agreement, of the same year, which was supposed to impose a voluntary restriction of imports from the Empire, did not, in fact, result in any diminution of the flow.

Other protective legislation was enacted as the 1930s progressed. The Wheat Act of 1934 imposed a small import levy on imported wheat to help provide a subsidy on home-grown wheat, in an effort to increase the wheat acreage. The 1933 Agricultural Marketing Act provided the Board of Trade with the power to restrict imports when desirable. The 1937 Agriculture Act introduced, as a measure of help to home farmers in their struggle against overseas competition, subsidies on barley and oats, an increase in the quantity of wheat available for subsidy, and subsidies on lime and basic slag.

The two Agricultural Marketing Acts, those of 1931 and 1933, dealt not only with imports but with the regulation of home supplies. Under them marketing boards, the first being the Milk Marketing Board, were set up. By the outbreak of war marketing boards had been established for pigs, potatoes and hops.

THE SITUATION IN 1939

By 1939 therefore the situation on the farm showed a modest improvement over the beginning of the decade. Agriculture was gradually becoming better organized, was being more sympathetically regarded in at least some official circles, and was sharing in the general improvement in prosperity.

Nevertheless, it was still a desperately needy industry. Since 1875, more than sixty years earlier, the only real period of prosperity it had known was the brief interlude of the 1914–18 War. It had then, of course, been handicapped by the innumerable worries and exigencies of war, and it had been plunged into depression again almost before it had recovered.

Consequently the farms were exhausted. Millions of acres of formerly arable land were lying derelict, the haunts of even more millions of rabbits. Hedges were unkempt and fences broken down. Nearly all the better farm buildings dated from the great Victorian era of expansion, between 1845 and 1875, and many of them were sadly in need of thatch and nails, let alone modernization. The sheep population of England and Wales had fallen by over four millions since the 1870s. Farm wages stood at 35s. a week. Farm land was bought for as little as £3 an acre, and for scores of thousands of acres of tenant farms no tenant could be found, even when they were offered for several years rent-free.

On this debilitated industry fell the task of producing the greater part of the food required by an industrial nation engaged in a desperate war. In 1939 we were importing over 70% of our food and growing less than 30%, and this proportion had as far as possible to be reversed.

THE WAR AGRICULTURAL EXECUTIVE COMMITTEES

One of the first steps was the establishment of the War Agricultural Executive Committees, who became for the next six years virtual agricultural dictators in their respective districts. Their duty was to direct farm production along the lines of official policy, encouraging maximum output and dealing ruthlessly, even to the extent of dispossession, with any farmer unwilling or unable to co-operate.

A feature of agriculture in 1939 was the preponderance of grass, accounting for 60% of the total farm area, but not including rough grazing. Much of the grass was old, poor stuff, ripe for ploughing up. It was realized that such old swards constituted a reservoir of fertility, and one of the primary aims of wartime agricultural policy was therefore to cash in on that reserve. By the end of the war 5,500,000 acres of old grassland had been reclaimed for arable crop production, increasing our home-grown food supplies by more than 70%.

This was only one facet of the wartime agricultural revolution. Under Lend-Lease a flow of American farm machinery began to replace, at an accelerating rate, the traditional horses and worn-out implements with which the British farmer worked. The increased use of improved chemical fertilizers resulted in more abundant yields, not only from arable crops but from the remaining grass. In spite of the vast reduction in pasture area, milk supplies actually rose (by about 100,000 gallons a year) during the war period.

FARMING IN 1945

Although the effort had been prodigious and expensive, British agriculture was in a far healthier state at the end of the war than it had been at any time since the early 1870s. Through the bounty poured in from America, it was far better equipped with machinery than any other European country. Moreover, although war-weary, the British farmer had a more progressive outlook than his European counterpart. For six years he had been geared to maximum production, receptive to new ideas and technical advice and co-operative with authority. For the same period the European farmer, in practically every country outside devastated Germany, had been not only starved of ideas and equipment, but had grown to identify low production and non-cooperation with patriotism. Such habits of thought are not changed overnight.

British farmers thus had a flying start in producing food to help meet the world shortage.

Jeremiahs were not wanting, however, to prophesy woe. Drawing conclusions from the analogy of the First World War, they declared that by 1948 the lessons of the Second World War would have faded and that British farming, abandoned once again to meet the demands of world trade, would be hurtling headlong towards yet another depression. The passing of the 1947 Agriculture Act did nothing to dispel their gloom. After all, the Corn Production Act of 1918 had been repealed after three years.

Yet there were several important differences from the 1920 situation, of which they had failed to take account. Of these the most important were:

(*a*) the tremendous increase in world population, some of it in awakening countries able to provide alternative markets for the available food;

(*b*) a better appreciation by the Government of the military value of agriculture;

(*c*) the continuance of the Cold War.

This last was perhaps the most important of all. At the end of the Second World War, although the peoples of the world yearned more deeply than ever for an era of universal peace, few of them had any illusions about its imminence.

THE 1947 AGRICULTURE ACT

The 1947 Agriculture Act was not repealed, but has remained the basis of British agricultural policy to the time of writing. Chief of its provisions are guaranteed prices for most farm commodities, though these are in some instances linked with statutory quantities. The prices, which may not vary by more than a small fixed percentage annually, are determined each year at a price review, at which the Ministry of Agriculture discusses them with representatives of the farmers. When the market price for any commodity falls below the guaranteed price, the difference is made up by the Government, a system which has in recent years involved the Government in huge subsidies. It must be remembered, however, that their level can be controlled by the Government by the simple expedient of restricting imports, which bring down the market price. Both leading political parties, however, prefer the payment of farm subsidies to the reduction of imports. The 1947 Act and subsequent ones also provide for the encouragement of progressive farming by a wide range of subsidies on fertilizers, equipment, weed control, livestock improvement, amenity installations, buildings and so on.

THE NATIONAL AGRICULTURAL ADVISORY SERVICE

The War Agricultural Executive Committees were in wartime composed mainly of farmers aided by a technical staff provided by the Ministry of Agriculture. Afterwards the two were split. The Agricultural Executive Committees still exist, though with limited functions, but the technical staff, now organized as the National Agricultural Advisory Service, continue to play a most important role in farming. Their officers are trained not only to give technical advice on particular problems but managerial advice on the economic running of farms, and their services are commonly in demand by the great majority of farmers.

THE EUROPEAN COMMON MARKET

The post-war technical developments of farming we shall discuss in later chapters, but to bring the background story up to date we must mention here the European Common Market.

Just before the fall of France in 1940 Winston Churchill dramatically offered the French common citizenship if they would fight on, but after the war nothing came of this vision. The idea of European unity was, however, growing, and in 1957 was crystallized by the Treaty of Rome, which set up the European Economic Community. The idea was to weld the six signatory countries, namely France, West Germany, Italy, Belgium, the Netherlands and Luxembourg, into one economic unit. The eventual aim is to eliminate all tariff barriers between them, resulting in complete free trade, and to admit from outside only such commodities as cannot be produced within the group or such others as are jointly agreed upon. For this policy to be effective, both prices and costs of production need to be approximately the same for each member country. This requires decreases in some prices, increases in others and a general raising of wages and standards of living in some of the poorer regions. The problem is being tackled industry by industry and commodity by commodity, and the process is gradual.

When it became apparent that the idea was likely to succeed Britain had the alternatives of remaining outside and watching an increasing barrier to her trade being erected just across the Channel, or of applying for membership of the European Economic Community. In 1961 it chose the latter course, and throughout most of 1962 negotiations slowly proceeded.

One of the chief difficulties (although there were others equally important but less publicized) lay with agriculture. The countries of the Common Market maintained that the British system of guaranteed prices supported by subsidies was incompatible with the system they were striving to establish. Differences were being patiently ironed out and success seemed near when, early in 1963, President de Gaulle of France, who evidently had no intention of allowing Britain into a Community which he hoped to dominate, bluntly brought the negotiations to an end.

There for a moment the matter rests. It certainly will not do so indefinitely. In due course negotiations will doubtless be resumed and we shall take our place in the European Economic Community. The delay may in the end prove to have been beneficial. The six countries already inside are having their own difficulties over agricultural adjustments, and opinion is strengthening that our system of subsidies and guaranteed prices may be the best, after all. On the other hand, in Britain itself there is a growing demand, though its strength is as yet uncertain, to reduce and eventually abandon subsidies and replace them by tariffs and import control.

THE PRESENT SITUATION

Meantime agriculture in Britain continues to flourish on the whole, though not to the same extent as urban industries and with many exceptions among individual farmers. It is an age of specialization and mass production in agriculture as in other industries. Large units do well, while small mixed farms of the traditional type find life increasingly difficult.

At the moment the situation is dominated by a world surplus of food, at least in the countries which can afford to buy it. This state of affairs can be only temporary. As populations increase almost beyond the powers of imagination and as the new emergent countries of the world prosper sufficiently to provide profitable markets, so the time will arrive when, as in 1939–45, we shall need every bit of food we can produce on our own acres. But we shall look a little more closely at the future in our final chapter.

4

THE STORY OF THE SOIL

THE foundation of all agriculture is the comparatively
shallow coating of soil which covers part of the face of the
earth. In Britain this ranges in thickness from nil to ten or
more feet, as in the Fens. The Ministry of Agriculture's
statistics show about 24,400,000 acres of crops and grass in
England and Wales, plus a further 5,000,000 acres classified
as rough grazing. In Scotland, where the statistics are compiled rather differently, the total tillage acreage, including
permanent grass not intended for mowing, is about 4,300,000.
The total of nearly 34,000,000 acres is about the maximum
amount of agricultural land available in the island at present,
though it is not impossible that science will find a way of
creating more.

KEEPING THE LAND IN GOOD HEART

The story of how this immense area of land has been
brought into production and, more particularly, held in production we shall now trace. For not the least of the resounding
achievements of British agriculture is that it has succeeded in

keeping land in cultivation for several thousands of years and is now producing far heavier crops from it than ever before. Each of a long line of generations of farmers has added his contribution to the proverbial rural art of 'keeping the land in good heart'.

PRIMEVAL BRITAIN

Primeval Britain was a land of forests. Professor G. M. Trevelyan lyrically paints its picture:

'Its moist and mossy floor was hidden from heaven's eye by a closely-drawn curtain woven of innumerable tree-tops, which shivered in the breezes of summer dawn and broke into wild music of millions upon millions of wakening birds; the concert was prolonged from bough to bough with scarcely a break for hundreds of miles over hill and plain and mountain, unheard by man save where, at rarest intervals, a troop of skin-clad hunters, stone-axe in hand, moved furtively over the ground beneath, ignorant that they lived upon an island, not dreaming that there could be other parts of the world besides this damp green woodland with its meres and marshes, wherein they hunted, a terror to its four-footed inhabitants and themselves afraid. . . .'

From this world of trees the chalk hills of southern and eastern England emerged like islands. Here the early shepherd tribes pastured their flocks, and here the first tentative experiments in growing crops were made.

Authorities summarize the climatic conditions of Britain for the last ten thousand years B.C. as follows. Ice ages ebbed and flowed until the ice cap finally began to retreat from Scotland about 7800 B.C. There followed two thousand years of warm, dry weather, known as the Boreal Period, during which the typical vegetation of temperate Europe spread steadily northwards. Britain, then still joined to the Continent, had a very sparse population of hunters.

In the Atlantic Period, extending over the next three thousand years (and thus taking the story to about 2500 B.C.), the climate was still warm, but became much wetter, and the forests flourished. During this long expanse of years Britain was finally severed from the Continent and was also invaded by new tribes which we call Neolithic. These men were not only hunters but kept domestic animals, as we briefly discussed earlier, and also brought with them cultivated plants. They settled on the dry hill slopes and scratched their tiny fields with primitive wooden implements and antlers.

From 2500 to about 500 B.C., the Sub-Boreal Period, the climate became drier. The thin, pervious soils on the crests of the chalk hills evidently became too dry for cultivation, which consequently moved downhill. New waves of invaders appearing from the Continent between 1000 and 500 B.C. probably introduced a light ox-plough and began the onslaught on the receding forest.

The Early Historical Period

About 500 B.C. began the Sub-Atlantic Period of somewhat cooler, damper weather in which, with minor variations, we still live. Rachel Carson, in *The Sea Around Us*, linking the climate of north-western Europe with a rhythmic cycle of tides, suggests that the cycle is one of eighteen centuries. Thus a period of maximum tidal activity, bringing storm and cold and 'a great invasion of the ocean', drove many tribes from their homes around the Baltic Sea between 500 and 300 B.C. and upset the stability of Europe. Brennus and his invading Celts are reputed to have sacked Rome in 391 B.C. Nine hundred years after that bring us to a period of minimum activity, about A.D. 400–600. During this epoch the seas around northern Europe seem to have been calm enough for abundant traffic. The Anglo-Saxon tribes crossed wholesale to colonize Britain, the Celtic saints ranged from Iceland to Madeira in their curraghs, and, a little later, the Norsemen felt their way into the White Sea and across the North Atlantic to Greenland and America.

Another nine hundred years, taking the story to the four-teenth century A.D., sees the Greenland colonies being over-whelmed by ice, the Baltic frozen over, and numerous European records of storms and catastrophes. By this reckon-ing, says Miss Carson, we are now approaching a period of minimum tidal activity with tranquil seas and an equable climate which should be at its best about A.D. 2400. Although we are frequently tempted to comment that we see few signs of this, the theory, objectively considered, seems a sound one.

Returning to the beginning of this Sub-Atlantic Period, the invasions of Britain by Celtic tribes, which started then, con-tinued until the first century B.C., when the Belgae came over from northern France. This tribe, establishing itself in south-eastern Britain, is now supposed to have brought with it the heavy ox-plough equipped with a mould-board for turning a furrow. By means of this implement men were enabled at last to tackle the heavier soils. Cultivation took dramatic bites out of the enveloping forests, and, as we have seen, in the period immediately prior to the Roman invasion, Britain was actually exporting grain.

In passing, it may be mentioned that those hillside terraces known as lynchets, which are a feature of so many chalk land-scapes, are now generally supposed to belong to the Celtic period. It is thought, though by no means proven, that they may have been formed by contour ploughing with a mould-board plough which consistently turned its furrow downhill.

The Earliest Cultivations

We have now arrived at a period when much of the better soil was in more or less permanent use. In earlier epochs cultivation was intermittent and desultory. For instance, Pro-fessor V. Gordon Childe, in *The Prehistory of European Society*, describes the early Neolithic culture of the Balkans as follows :

'Perhaps these villagers had learned a system of rotation; to clear patches of forest with fire, to allow scrub to grow again when the soil showed signs of exhaustion, and then to burn off the brushwood once more; the ash layer left by each burning acts as a fertilizer and permits the growth of a new crop on the same patch. This system requires a lot of land, since plots must be left fallow for seven or more years and throughout that time must be protected from grazing stock. . . .'

Tacitus has this to say about the much later Germans of his day (the second half of the first century A.D.):

'They change their plough-lands yearly, and still there is ground to spare. The fact is that their soil is fertile and plentiful, but they refuse to give it the labour it deserves. They plant no orchards, fence off no meadows, water no gardens; the only levy on the earth is the corn crop. . . .'

Both present pictures of a rural civilization in which land appears to be an unlimited commodity. The attitude of the tribesmen is that of the earliest exploiters of America's Middle West. They break up the virgin soil, crop it until it shows signs of exhaustion, and then move on.

The system is sound enough. Given time, soil will replenish its resources. The debris of each autumn is rotted into humus, in which micro-organisms thrive. In our own time the farmers of the early 1940s were surprised at the fertility stored in grassland which had remained derelict throughout the long depression.

THE ADVENT OF SEDENTARY FARMERS

We have in the above quotations, however, an indication of two alternative methods of land exploitation. In one the cultivators are on the move. They take their crops and move on. In the other they are sedentary. When they cease cultivating a plot of land they have every intention of returning to it later, and so they take steps to nourish it and protect it. They erect fences to keep their livestock from grazing it prematurely, and they occasionally burn the grass or scrub to enrich the soil, an operation the advantage of which can easily be established by observation.

In Britain immediately before the Roman invasion this second phase seems to have been widespread, though only in the south-eastern sector was there any large-scale cultivation. The north was probably devoted almost entirely to stock-rearing. The Romans imposed a more rigid pattern on the countryside, based on a network of small towns. At the height of the Roman era, according to Professor L. Dudley Stamp, 'the area cultivated and cropped cannot have been less than a million acres, and may well have been nearer 4,000,000. In addition were the sheep and cattle pastures. These figures we may apply to lowland England alone; too little is known of Wales and Scotland. Already then some 10 to 20 per cent. of the surface of England was cultivated . . .'

Roman writers, notably Varro, Pliny and Virgil, reveal a knowledge of the soil and its needs which is, in many respects, quite up to date. They were familiar with various types of soil, such as clay, sand, gravel and stony; and they even differentiated between soils acid and alkaline. More particularly, they knew how to improve soils both by a system of alternate husbandry and by manuring.

Sings Virgil:

> Land by flax and oats
> Exhausted, is consumed where slumber-steeped
> Poppies of Lethe lift their glowing heads.
> Natheless, by change of crops is labour eased;
> Only be not ashamed with fattening dung
> To enrich dry soil, or, when its life is gone,
> To foul your hands by scattering wood-ash.
> So will rotation rest your land: meanwhile
> There is no loss through acres left untilled. . . .

Again, Dr A. C. Bouquet, writing of the Roman world in his *Everyday Life in New Testament Times*, refers to the Roman writers as giving 'very careful instructions about the different

23 Champion Hereford, Shropshire and West Midlands Show, 1964.

24 Champion British Friesian Cow at the Shropshire and West
Midlands Show, 1964.

25 Champion Northern Dairy Shorthorn Cow at Carlisle Show, 1957

26 Supreme **Pair** of Pigs—Welsh Heavies—at the Royal Smithfiel
Show, 1963.

sorts of manure, including bird guano, with which they are quite familiar, and also instructions for the making of compost heaps, to which are added ashes, road scrapings and sweepings from the house, as well as leaves, hedge clippings and straw. They know well the system of manuring by penning and feeding sheep upon a limited space of ground, the quantities of dung to be used for spreading on different kinds of land, and also the use of marl, containing a large quantity of phosphate of lime.'

Shortcomings of Roman Rule

Much of this knowledge doubtless came to Rome from the more ancient civilizations of the East, and how much of it filtered through to Britain is doubtful. The indications are that the Romans took little trouble to teach the Britons anything so fundamentally practical as improved farming methods. Rather, they were content to name their heavy tribute and leave the natives to produce it as best they could. Archaeologists have searched mostly in vain for evidences, which they were once convinced must exist, of fields and estates laid out by Roman mensuration. Even in the Fens, once the main dykes were planned, the oppressed Iceni were left to reclaim and cultivate the land according to their own devices, provided they satisfied the demands of the Roman tax-collector.

Nevertheless, during the four hundred years of Roman rule, when the population of the country may well have risen to 1,500,000, even the humble British peasants of the Wessex downlands and the Welsh valleys must have learned something from their Roman overlords. In their heyday the estates of Romano-British villas in southern England must have been very similar to the estates of eighteenth-century gentry. The fields were doubtless farmed in accordance with the principles of sound husbandry and tended by workmen who, although perhaps slaves, understood the finer points of the arts of cultivation.

F.I.B.—E

The Coming of the Saxons

When the lights went out over Europe these arts were largely obliterated and had to be re-learnt by new nations. The Saxon farmer came equipped with certain advantages. He possessed a heavy plough, drawn by as many as eight oxen on stiff soil, and he had an instinct for the best soils. The open downland with its shallow covering of humus did not tempt him, and his experience showed him which were the unproductive gravels. Armed with axe and fire he cleared space for his homestead on the clays and loams by the rivers up which he had guided his boat.

It took some six hundred years for the population to climb again to its Roman level, but by the year of the Domesday Book it had reached it approximately, a careful estimate of the population of England and Wales in 1086 being 1,200,000. We have already seen that with a population of this density there is no scope for nomadic or haphazard farming. It calls for a carefully ordered and strictly applied social structure, such as now developed as the feudal system.

The Open-field System

We have already taken note of the organization of the parish during these centuries, but must briefly consider the effects of the open-field system on the soil. It contained the rudiments of alternate husbandry. After two harvests, one of wheat and one of barley, each field was given a rest, during which it was sometimes grazed by the parish sheep and cattle. In addition, the village livestock, which thickly populated the commons, were allowed to forage on the stubbles after harvest. There was therefore some replenishment of the soil's fertility.

Some alternation of common with arable land may also have occurred, especially in the early part of the period. A. G. Tansley, in *Britain's Green Mantle*, points out that 'the extensive pasturing of cattle through forest always leads to the disappearance of woodland plants, consolidation of the soil through trampling, and the introduction of grass vegetation conditions which make the germination and establishment of tree seedlings more difficult, apart from their destruction by browsing, and thus lead to the disappearance of the forest as the old trees die'. Certainly cattle must have aided the process of reclamation from the waste.

However, the principle of common ownership and collective cultivation of the open fields militated against progress. Custom was doubtless supreme, with no rewards for original ideas. When custom ordained that wheat was to be sown in a certain field on a certain date, it was so sown, and no arguments. Nor was there any incentive for long-term improvements of the soil when, as apparently was the custom in some parishes, the individual strips in the open fields were reshuffled and dealt out to different owners after each harvest.

EARLY MEDIAEVAL CROP YIELDS

A book entitled *Anonymous Husbandry*, probably written in the first half of the thirteenth century, makes the following suggestions of the yields a good farmer might expect. Barley should increase 8-fold, rye 7-fold, wheat-rye 6-fold, wheat 5-fold, oats 4-fold. The writer gives seed rates at 2·4 bushels per acre for wheat, rye, beans and peas; and 4 bushels per acre for barley and oats. The yields are thus 32 bushels, or 8 cwt., per acre for barley; 16 bushels, or 6 cwt, per acre for oats; 12 bushels, or $6\frac{3}{4}$ cwt., for wheat; and 16·8 bushels, or 4·2 cwt., for rye. Doubtless the harvest of the average farmer was a good deal less than these figures indicate.

THE ROLE OF THE MONASTERIES

While the peasant groped slowly towards a better understanding of the principles of good husbandry, these were revived on the monastic and later the secular estates. We must remember that although the irruption of the barbarians during the Dark Ages obliterated most of the Roman science and culture from Britain, the destruction was not so complete in other parts of the Empire. The old lore and culture survived and produced seed which, when sown in new fields, quickly sprouted and brought forth a rich harvest.

While we know little of what went on in monastery gardens, the student cannot fail to be impressed by the large number of vegetables first mentioned in literature, and therefore presumed to have been introduced to England, in the sixteenth century. They include the leek (first mentioned in 1557), onion (reign of Elizabeth I), turnip (about 1550), radish (1548), pea (reign of Henry VIII), lettuce (1562), beetroot (1548), carrot (1558), globe artichoke (1546), endive (1548), gourd (1547), French bean (1509), parsley (1548), rhubarb (1573), sage (1573), spinach (1568), thyme (1548), as well as a further range of herbs apparently brought to England about the same time. Now, is it really true that these few decades in the middle of the sixteenth century saw all these vegetables and herbs in English gardens for the first time? Is it not more likely that they had been there for centuries, but that it was only with the Renaissance and the invention of printing that men began again to write about them? An indication that this is the correct explanation is to be found in the facts that (a) the cabbage was not mentioned in literature until the sixteenth century, although it had almost certainly been cultivated in England from time immemorial, and (b) the cucumber, which would otherwise be classified as a sixteenth-century introduction, is by chance mentioned in a document of 1327.

If mediaeval gardeners did indeed cultivate a fair range of vegetables and herbs, we may assume that they had a wider knowledge of the maintenance of soil fertility than did the peasants on the other side of the garden wall. One may guess that they had some knowledge of the making and use of compost and of the principles of crop rotation. Other items of

Roman lore may have survived. Did the monks know, for instance, of the old Roman custom of ploughing in broad beans, just before flowering, in order to manure the land? Pliny had mentioned it, declaring that it did as much good as a coating of manure. If gardeners understood this principle throughout the Middle Ages, we can understand how knowledge of it eventually escaped into the fields and became crystallized in the Norfolk four-course rotation. Red clover, like the vegetables just mentioned, first appears in literature in the sixteenth century, when it attracted a good deal of attention on the Continent and was introduced to England, it is thought, by Sir Richard Weston.

THE NORFOLK FOUR-COURSE ROTATION

The essential feature of the Norfolk four-course rotation is that it alternates a straw crop with a root or seeds crop. In its basic form it runs:

Roots – barley – seeds – wheat.

The roots were originally turnips and swedes. On light soils they were eaten by sheep folded on them; on heavier land they were sometimes carted to bullocks in yards, from which farmyard manure was returned to the fields. Either way they provided an abundance of animal food, though at the expense of a good deal of hand labour, and also a good manuring of the soil in readiness for the next crop, barley.

This spring-sown crop was undergrown with seeds, usually red clover with or without rye-grass. Sainfoin, trefoil and beans were used as alternatives in some districts. They normally yielded a hay crop, followed by an aftermath which was sometimes cut or grazed and sometimes ploughed in. Farmyard manure could, if time allowed, be spread on the sward before ploughing.

Although an infinite number of variations has since been developed on this theme, the principles behind the Norfolk four-course remain the foundations of modern husbandry.

Townshend and Coke

The Norfolk four-course was itself evolved to meet special conditions. Upon retiring from politics in 1730 the second Viscount Townshend set about improving his lands at Raynham, in Norfolk. His pioneering work was expanded, forty-six years later, by Thomas Coke, afterwards Earl of Leicester, on neighbouring estates at Holkham. The problem of these two notable farmers was a light, sandy, unproductive soil, which they proceeded to improve by two methods. They stiffened it by adding marl, which is fortunately found in the vicinity; and they enriched it with organic manure. The latter operation involved liberal applications of farmyard manure, which in turn implied the provision of crops to feed the animals. Roots were grown extensively for winter food, and the four-course rotation was devised to fit both them and the enriching clover into the cropping programme.

By the end of the eighteenth century, therefore, it was widely recognized by progressive farmers that plants require food and that the way to provide this in poor soils was to plough in both animal manure and green crops. The truth was not universally accepted, however. Jethro Tull, who published his classic, *The New Horse-Houghing Husbandry, or an Essay on the Principles of Tillage and Vegetation*, in 1731, was so enthusiastic about his experiments with seed-drills and horse-hoeing that he maintained that these alone were sufficient to maintain the fertility of the soil, manures being unnecessary.

Pioneers in Agricultural Chemistry

Many years earlier, in 1563, the French potter, Bernard Palissy, in the course of his experiments hit upon the truth that the part of farmyard manure which can be utilized by plants is that which is soluble in water. It was not until the development of agricultural chemistry, however, that the real facts of plant nutrition were understood. A farmer named

Boussingault, who experimented on his own fields at Bechel-bronne, Alsace, in the 1830s, discovered that plants fed on nitrogen in the soil and on carbon from the atmosphere. The founder of the science of agricultural chemistry was the great German chemist, Justus Liebig, who worked at Giessen and Munich from 1824 to 1873. He stated that the carbon compounds derivable from the atmosphere constitute 95% of the plant, which can obtain its other requirements from the same source if it is provided with about 2% of mineral constituents. Although he underestimated the value of nitrogen and overestimated the amount of nitrogen obtainable from rain, and although he did not properly understand the proportions needed of the various mineral constituents, his work has been the basis for almost all subsequent research.

Joseph Henry Gilbert, one of Liebig's chemists at Giessen, himself acquired a pupil, John Bennet Lawes, who began testing on the fields of his estate at Rothamsted, Hertfordshire, some of the new chemical theories. The genius of Lawes soon corrected Liebig's erroneous ideas on nitrogen, a fact vehemently resented by the German chemist. Lawes established a direct connection between crop yields and the amount of nitrogen applied. He showed that plants could not absorb free nitrogen from the air, but took it up in solution from the soil. He also determined which minerals were essential to plant growth, demonstrating the prime importance of potassium and phosphorus.

The use of manures supplying the essential plant foods antedated the scientific discovery of the part played by those substances. We have seen that generations of farmers understood that animal manure and later the refuse of green crops enriched the soil, although they knew nothing of nitrogen. Similarly, as far back at least as the seventeenth century and probably earlier such substances as blood, bones, wood ash, hoof parings, soot, fish, rags and wool were used as fertilizers, while the practice of paring and burning turf from banks and spreading the ash on fields was certainly known. More surprisingly, Mr W. G. T. Packard, in a paper delivered to the Fertiliser Society in 1952, stated that sulphate of ammonia was in steady demand in England by 1833, having been manufactured here since 1815.

Mineral Manures

Lawes in England and James Murray in Ireland were granted patents for the production of superphosphate on the same day (23rd May 1842), but Murray seems to have been manufacturing it at least a year previously, and Heinrich Kohler, in Bohemia, was producing a fertilizer by treating bone with sulphuric acid in 1831. The commercial enterprise started by Lawes in 1843 still flourishes.

In 1847 the coprolite deposits in Suffolk, Cambridgeshire and Bedfordshire were recognized as valuable sources of phosphate and began to be mined. In the next twenty years other geological sources were exploited in Norway, France, North Carolina and the West Indies. Since then nearly forty countries have engaged in phosphate mining, and in the last few years useful deposits have been discovered on the sea-bed off the Pacific coast fo America.

No major sources of potash were exploited till the Germans began to develop huge deposits at Stassfurt in 1875. These supplied the greater part of the world's needs till the 1930s. Since then commercial potash-extracting enterprises have flourished in California, Sicily, Canada, Yorkshire, Russia and elsewhere, and vast untapped resources are known to exist. While the Dead Sea is already yielding quantities of potash, the oceans themselves contain a significant amount of it (an average of 0·05%), which it may be eventually possible to extract economically.

Apart from farmyard manure, green crops and sulphate of ammonia, two of the sources of nitrogen exploited before the middle of the nineteenth century were the sodium-nitrate deposits of Chile and the guano from the bird islands of Peru.

Guano was imported to England in 1840 and Chilean nitrates a few years earlier.

Basic slag, a phosphatic manure, was discovered as a by-product of the Bessemer process for steel production. It was not used as a fertilizer until after 1885, when experiments in Wiltshire and Durham established its value.

'Artificial' and 'Natural' Fertilizers

Thus, following on the scientific discovery of plant nutrients and how they are absorbed, the nineteenth century witnessed the development of a whole range of fertilizers able to supply them. They are the chemical or 'artificial' fertilizers, in contrast to the organic or 'natural' fertilizers. Although it is difficult to draw a logical line of demarcation between them, the use of the new chemical fertilizers aroused some controversy, which still lingers. One school of thought maintains that the use of compost is infinitely preferable to that of mineral manures, and examples can be produced of quite large farms yielding adequate crops without the aid of chemical fertilizers. By and large, however, British agriculture readily uses all aids to increased production, and much of the credit for its immense achievements during and since the Second World War is due to the intelligent use of all types of fertilizers.

Until the late 1930s progress in the use of chemical fertilizers was desultory. Little by little their functions began to be appreciated. Farmers took to applying kainit to mangold crops, superphosphate to clover, sulphate of ammonia to cabbages and barley, and so on. Unfortunately, their increased availability coincided with the series of agricultural depressions. Increases in yields (theoretical to those who had never before tried such fertilizers) did not compensate for falling prices. Only naturally fertile land was worth keeping in production. The soils which would most have benefited from generous manuring fell into dereliction.

Compound Granulated Fertilizers

Moreover, the simple chemical manures were not easy to handle. Basic slag powdered its handlers with black dust till they looked like chimney-sweeps. Sulphate of ammonia in dampish, crystalline form was often sown by hand from a shoulder-slung seed-lip. The great advance in this field in the 1920s and 1930s was the development of granulated compound fertilizers. Made available in a wide range of compounds in which the proportions of nitrogen, phosphates and potassium were matched to specific crops or soils, these fertilizers were in full commercial production in time to play an essential role in averting famine during the Second World War.

Land Reclamation

The stage was now set for the reclamation of millions of acres which had fallen out of cultivation. The enforced idleness had enabled them to regain their fertility through the slow accumulation of humus from successive years of rough grass and other wild vegetation, and now adequate supplies of manufactured fertilizers were ready to supplement the humus and to maintain production from the soil indefinitely. Other factors than manures had, however, a part to play in the exploitation of these neglected acres, and these we must consider before surveying the agricultural revolution of the 1940s.

Before we do so, let us briefly retrace our steps over the meadows, moors and marshes of Britain and recapitulate the stages by which they have been won for the service of man. First, the thin soils of the open hills, mostly on the chalk, were grazed, cultivated and later abandoned for better soil. Through long centuries the dense carpet of trees was cleared from most of lowland Britain and the land made to produce crops. In recent times, when each parish ceased to be entirely dependent on its own resources, specialization increased, some districts becoming renowned for wheat, others for fattening pastures and so on. Concurrently men were learning how to increase the productivity of their local soils by sound methods of husbandry and by the aid of new allies, such as chemical fertilizers. There were, however, special areas where something more was needed and in due course supplied. Most important of these was the Fens.

THE FENS

This great region, extending some seventy miles from south of Ely to Wainfleet and covering much of Cambridgeshire, Lincolnshire, the Marshland division of Norfolk, and parts of Northamptonshire, Huntingdonshire and Suffolk, lay so flat that the Midland rivers lost themselves on their way to the sea. Disorientated among the reeds, they staggered aimlessly this way and that, now expanding into almost stagnant meres, now encompassing marshy islands. The whole amphibious kingdom was alive with waterfowl and fish, not to mention a quite substantial human population who derived a living from them.

Little remained of the extensive Roman work when the Earl of Bedford, and afterwards his son, the first Duke of Bedford, began their ambitious reclamation schemes in the seventeenth century. Advised by the Dutch expert, Vermuyden, they slashed across the old tortuous waterways the straight Old Bedford River, twenty-one miles long and 70 feet wide. Twenty years later the New Bedford River was cut parallel to this, and thereafter the reclamation of the Fens progressed rapidly, though vigorously opposed by the marshmen, who saw their livelihood disappearing.

A new set of problems inherent in these large drainage schemes was solved in the late seventeenth and eighteenth centuries. It was found that this flat province did not drain itself naturally, even when adequate channels were provided. The black, peaty soils in particular shrank when drained, their level falling as they dried out. Consequently water had to be pumped up from the fields into the drainage ditches and from the drainage ditches to the main channels. The early solution to the problem was to instal innumerable windmills for the task, these being replaced in the nineteenth century by steam-driven pumps and now by diesel or electric engines. Sluice-gates at the river mouths also prevented the sea at high tide from forcing back the river water and causing it to flood the fields.

Capital as a New Factor in Reclamation

Professor G. M. Trevelyan, in his *English Social History*, underlines the essential difference between this magnificent achievement and the general pattern of farming history. The new Fenland province, he writes, 'had not, like the older fields of England, been won from the waste by the gradual encroachment of innumerable peasants and landowners, diligently working through centuries to increase bit by bit each his own estate. The victory over nature in Fenland was due to the accumulation of capital and its application to an enterprise conceived beforehand on a large scale by men who were ready to risk great sums of money and wait twenty years or more for a return.' Francis, Earl of Bedford, indeed invested from first to last at least £100,000 in the venture.

Similar but much less extensive schemes have reclaimed marches in Lancashire, Kent, South Wales and elsewhere, but there is still scope for more.

Two other adventures in reclaiming land from watery wastes deserve mention, though they have operated on a much smaller scale.

Warping

One is the creation of new land by warping. This is, in effect, the building up of new fields from silt deposited near the mouths of rivers. The requirement is a swift-flowing river bringing a sizeable burden of silt from mountains, as the Nile does. In England the outstanding example is the Humber.

Tide-covered riparian marshes are enclosed by an earthen embankment through which certain tides are admitted, by narrow channels controlled by sluices. As the tide ebbs it leaves a deposit, about the thickness of a penny, of mud. Over a period of several years, using only carefully selected tides, a fertile soil eighteen inches deep is built up. The process is expensive, though modern earth-shifting machinery has made it more economical, but the fields thus won are so rich that they normally require no further manuring for a generation.

Water-meadows

The other enterprise was the reclamation of the riverside meadows of southern England by means of irrigation channels. Here it is correct to speak in the past tense, for, although occasional schemes for warping are still undertaken, almost all the water-meadows were laid out in the eighteenth century – indeed, I know of none that have been created since.

Pioneer of the principle is stated to have been one Squire Baverstock, of Stockton, in the Wylye valley of Wiltshire, who flourished early in the eighteenth century. Much of the engineering is reputed to have been done by 'Dutchmen', which seems likely enough.

These experts took a cross-section of rough, marshy meadow on either side of the river and dug a series of parallel channels longitudinally, about four or five yards apart. These channels were at two levels: the 'carriages' ran along the top of a slight bank, their surface level with the water in the main stream above the meadow; the 'drains', arranged alternately with the 'carriages', were two or three feet lower.

At the head of the meadow a dam controlled the water-level and created a deep pool. When the meadows were flooded the hatches in the dam were opened sufficiently to allow water to flow brimming into the 'carriages' and spill over their rims. It then trickled down the gentle slope into the drains, which led it to the dam above the next meadow.

By the end of the eighteenth century most southern streams, especially on the chalk, had their valleys filled from end to end with this sort of water-meadow. The water was thus used time and again for irrigation, though when necessary strict regulations concerning quantities and dates were enforced.

Though expensive to create and calling for careful maintenance, exercised by skilled artists known as 'drowners', these meadows were extremely productive. Flooded in winter, usually from December to March, they provided irrigation not against drought but against frost. Beneath the quietly flowing carpet of water the grass continued to grow even during severe weather and was ready for grazing in March or early April. Thereafter the meadows were in constant use, either for grazing or for mowing, throughout the summer. Before the regular use of chemical fertilizers on pastures the system could hardly be matched.

The disappearance of sheep, during the years of depression, from the southern valleys caused the water-meadows to be neglected. Although the grass can, of course, be used equally well by cattle, their heavier hooves cause considerable damage to the channels and hence frequently upset the delicately adjusted levels. Also, the corrugated nature of the surface of the meadows precludes the use of machinery, either for maintenance or for mowing the grass.

Nevertheless, costings taken on some of the few surviving meadows have shown that they produce grass at about the same cost as do upland leys which rely on chemical fertilizers, and they can in most seasons produce an earlier bite. So any farmers who possess old water-meadows may find it profitable to maintain or even to revive them, though to create new ones would probably be prohibitively expensive.

Where old water-meadows have been allowed to fall derelict they have reverted to rush-infested wastes which have until recently defied efforts to reclaim them by other methods. In the past few years, however, some farmers have tackled the problem by lowering the bed of the river.

5

THE STORY OF OUR CROPS

Comparative acreages – Barley – Wheat – Spring wheats and winter barleys – Oats – Rye – Potatoes – Sugar-beet – Peas – Market gardens – Broad beans – Hops – Flax – Grasses – The Welsh Plant Breeding Station – Wild white clover – After the ploughing-up campaign – Turnips – Swedes – Mangolds – Cabbages and other brassicas – Fodder beet – Maize – Lucerne and other leguminous crops

COMPARATIVE ACREAGES

Of the 29,600,000 acres of land devoted to crops, grass and rough grazing in England and Wales, cereals, in the year 1962–3, which is the latest for which statistics are available at the time of writing, accounted for 6,665,000 acres. Barley occupied 3,501,000 acres; wheat 2,144,000 acres; oats 784,000 acres; mixed corn 119,000 acres; and rye 17,000 acres. Grass, both temporary and permanent but excluding what are classified as rough grazings, covered over 15,000,000 acres. Other important crops were potatoes (518,000 acres), sugar-beet (406,000 acres), turnips, swedes and fodder beet for stock-feeding (169,000 acres), kale (299,000 acres), mangolds (99,000 acres), peas (23,000 acres), and hops (20,000 acres).

BARLEY

Barley is thus, apart from grass, the largest crop we grow, and both its acreage and its yield are constantly increasing. Its importance until comparatively recent years has been relatively less. Although 'barley bannocks' were occasionally eaten by labourers within living memory, Englishmen, as many European travellers noted with some surprise, expected to eat wheaten bread. Wheat was for making bread, barley for beer, and oats, in the north, for porridge.

Since the influx of wheat from the sun-drenched prairies of North America we have been educated to believe that British wheat does not make good bread, or at least that our softer wheats have to be mixed with the flinty berries of these sun-baked imports. I suspect that modern milling machinery has been evolved to deal with that type of wheat rather than ours. Nevertheless, British farmers have little cause for complaint, for the millers usually manage to take most of their wheat for bread, and the price is guaranteed. The significance here is that our former reliance on home-grown wheat is past; we need only a limited quantity for our own consumption.

What we do need is an almost unlimited quantity of reasonably cheap cereals for feeding livestock, and for this purpose barley is more suitable than wheat. Many barley-growers still aim to produce samples of high-quality grain for the traditional malting, this normally commanding the highest prices, but most of us have to be content with the feeding-barley market. Much is produced for consumption on the farm which grows it. The barley acreage has increased from 2,120,000 acres in 1956 (to take a year more or less at random) to 3,501,000 acres at present, and is still climbing.

We have already noted that both six-row and two-row barleys were grown in Britain in prehistoric times. In the Near East barley was cultivated at least 10,000 years ago; even 50,000 years ago has been suggested. Wild forms of the genus *Hordeum*, from one or more of which our modern barleys derive, are still found from Syria to Central Asia. Our cultivated barleys are now classified under two main species, *Hordeum polystichum*, the six-rowed barley, and *Hordeum distichum*, the two-rowed barley.

The origins of the various types of barley from which our modern varieties have been evolved are lost in time. One of the earliest English writers to deal with the subject,

27 Wessex Saddle-back Sow and litter.

28 Champion Dartmoor Ram.

29   Dorset Horn Sheep from Mr J. Lenthall's Manor Farm, Burton
Bradstock, Dorset. The two nearer to the camera are naturally polled

30   Hampshire Down ram lambs.

Edward Lisle, of Crux Easton, in Hampshire, notes three types, in 1707, classified apparently according to the date of ripening. Rath-ripe barley, which ripened early, he found unsatisfactory on his light chalkland. Middle-ripe was not much better. Late-ripe he cultivated successfully. He also knew Spratt barley, though he did not cultivate it, considering it to be more suited to the rich soils of the eastern counties (he mentions Bedfordshire).

Dr E. S. Beaven, the father of barley-breeding, who worked at Warminster for many years subsequent to 1878, attempts to identify these types. The rath-ripe he considers similar to a strain grown in Ireland and known there as 'Old Irish', and to another grown on the Continent and known as 'Hanna'. Middle-ripe was probably a mixture of the former and a late barley. Late-ripe seems to have been the old English narrow-eared barley, widely grown and often known as 'Archer'.

In addition, Scotland had a barley of its own, known as 'Scotch Common'.

The story of one of the first experiments in improved barley-breeding is told in a paper written by Arthur Young, secretary to the Board of Agriculture from 1793 to 1808.

'About the year 1820, John Andrews, a labourer of Mr Edward Dove, of Ulverston Hall, Debenham (in Suffolk), had been threshing barley and on his return home at night complained of his feet being very uneasy, and on taking off his shoes he discovered in one of them part of a very fine ear of barley – it struck him as being particularly so – and he was careful to have it preserved. He afterwards planted the few grains from it in his garden, and the following year Dr and Mrs Charles Chevallier, coming to Andrews's dwelling to inspect some repairs going on (the cottage belonged to the Doctor), saw three or four ears of the barley growing. He requested it might be kept for him when ripe. The Doctor sowed a small ridge with the produce thus obtained, and kept it by itself until he grew sufficient to plant an acre, and from this acre the produce was 11½ coombs (about the year 1825 or

1826). This was again planted and from the increase thence arising, he began to dispose of it, and from that time it has been gradually getting into repute.'

(A coomb, by the way, is four bushels, so the yield was probably the excellent one of 23 cwt. per acre.)

This was the barley which, known as Chevalier, dominated the barley-growing scene for the rest of the century. An improvement on it was the variety Goldthorpe, grown from a single ear of Chevalier found in a field at Goldthorpe, Yorkshire, by a Mr Dyson in 1889. At least, the ear was found in a field of Chevalier, though whether it was an unusually fine example of that variety or a chance ear of Spratt barley or some other variety is not known. Goldthorpe was widely grown in the North and in the Lowlands of Scotland just before the First World War.

In the eighteen-nineties Dr E. S. Beaven began collecting barleys at his nursery at Warminster. Some had previously been sent him from Denmark, where similar experimental work was in progress, and now he started to buy specimens of Spratt barley from many districts, particularly from the Fens and Ireland.

In Ireland Dr H. Hunter was busy on similar work. He, like the Danes, concentrated on a type of barley known as Archer.

In 1901 the paper describing the painstaking research undertaken by the monk Gregor Mendel in Moravia in the middle of the nineteenth century was re-discovered in Brno. Appreciation of Mendel's laws of heredity gave a new impetus to scientific study of plant breeding and a better understanding of what might be done by hybridization.

In 1905 by cross-fertilization Dr Beaven produced, from his selected strains, the parents of Plumage-Archer barley. Three years later Dr Hunter, crossing some of Beaven's Spratt barleys with his own improved Archer stock, bred the equally celebrated Spratt-Archer.

These two varieties rapidly superseded Chevalier. From

1887 to 1890 Dr Beaven records that 83% of the named barleys entered for the barley competitions of the Brewers' Exhibition were Chevalier. From 1926 to 1936 Chevalier comprised only 2%. The National Institute of Agricultural Botany when it began its seed-testing work in 1922 found that, of 1,000–2,000 samples, 25% were of Spratt-Archer, Plumage-Archer or nearly allied varieties. By 1939 the proportion had risen to 88·9%. Dr Beaven was being modest when he claimed, during the war, that more than 85% of the barley then grown in Britain was the progeny of four plants, three of which were bred by him at Warminster between the years 1900 and 1904.

Since then new varieties have been evolved. A leading part has been played by the Plant Breeding Institute at Cambridge, presided over first by Dr H. Hunter and latterly by Dr G. D. H. Bell, who introduced in 1952 the variety Proctor, which proceeded to capture the greater part of the British acreage.

Valuable work has also been done by certain commercial houses which maintain plant-breeding stations, such as that of Messrs Nickerson at Rothwell, in Lincolnshire, but we tend to rely extensively on the plant-breeding work done by European breeders. Thus, among barleys, Rika and Freja were bred in Sweden, Cambrinus and Vada in the Netherlands, and Swallow in Germany. The state of affairs exists largely because British breeders have no legal rights over the plants they introduce and cannot, as in many other countries, draw royalties on them. A committee appointed by the Government in 1960 recommended in their report that breeders should be allowed to exercise such rights, to bring them into line with Continental practice, but at the time of writing no action has resulted.

In the past year or two a Swedish variety, Pallas, has leapt into popularity, accounting in 1963 for 40% of the total barley crop. This is the first commercial variety bred with the aid of radiation.

Wheat

The work of Beaven and Hunter on barley was paralleled by that of Sir Rowland Biffen on wheat.

With wheat the available material was more diverse than with barley. At least five types of wheat were cultivated in northern Europe in Neolithic times. In *The Practical Farmer or The Hertfordshire Husbandman*, William Ellis in 1732 mentioned four that were commonly grown locally. They were Old Red Lammas, which produced the finest flour and did best on rich land; Yellow Lammas, with a red ear and white straw, considered to be second-best; Pirky Wheat, 'the most convenient for our Chiltern lands'; and Dugdale Wheat, a hardy, square-headed wheat which did well on 'sour' soil.

Old Red Lammas may have been similar to Red Fife, a strong milling wheat used by Biffen in one of his first experiments in hybridization. By crossing it with a high-yielding variety of indifferent quality, named Rough Chaff, he achieved, by years of selection of the best progeny, a new and improved variety known as Burgoyne's Fife.

Biffen then attempted to cross the hard, strong wheats of Canada and Australia with some of the traditional English wheats. After some years of ruthless selection he bred, by 1916, the variety Yeoman, which in due course became as popular as Spratt-Archer and Plumage-Archer did among barleys.

From Yeoman the variety Holdfast was bred by Professor Engledow, who crossed it with White Fife. It, too, won its quota of popularity.

More recently other wheats have come to the fore, the present (1963) dominant variety being the French-bred Cappelle Desprez. This is now beginning to reveal weaknesses, notably a susceptibility to eyespot, and breeders are searching for a successor. Viking, Professor Marchal, Champlein and a new Nickerson variety dubbed Perdix are all challengers, but the outstanding wheat to sweep the board, as Proctor did in barley, has probably not yet appeared.

Modern wheats have not only to yield well but to stand up well for the combine-harvester, a requirement more difficult of fulfilment because of the response of wheat to nitrogen, which adds considerably to the yield but weakens the straw. For this reason the old varieties such as Squarehead's Master and Little Joss have been unable to meet modern conditions, and plant-breeders have to concentrate strongly on varieties with short, stiff straw. The wheat-breeder's career is also a ceaseless battle against fungus diseases, notably loose smut, eyespot and yellow rust.

SPRING WHEATS AND WINTER BARLEYS

Traditionally, wheat is an autumn-sown crop and barley a spring-sown. Soon after the war certain varieties of spring wheat were introduced, chiefly from France and Scandinavia, and several became popular. Outstanding was the Swedish-bred Atle, which was in the 1950s extensively grown in southern England. It has since been largely though not entirely superseded by Jufy I (from Belgium), Koga II and Opal (both German-bred), and several others. A 1963 catalogue on my desk lists seventeen varieties of spring wheat.

Nearly coincidental with the introduction of spring wheat was that of winter barley. The first and indeed the only outstanding variety so far on the market has been Pioneer, bred at Cambridge by Dr G. D. H. Bell in the late 1930s and introduced in 1943. It is of good quality, up to malting standard, as well as being hardy. Dea, a German variety introduced very recently, is, although a heavy yielder, so exceedingly coarse and fibrous as to be at times almost unmarketable. I have grown over 50 cwt. per acre of this variety, but have found harvesting very heavy work indeed.

The advantage of spring wheats and winter barleys is that they give the farmer greater latitude of cropping. In an open autumn after an early harvest he can deal with a proportion of his barley acreage, thus reducing the stockpile of work for the other end of the winter. Alternatively, if a wet autumn makes wheat-sowing impossible, as has happened quite frequently since the war, he can sow spring varieties.

OATS

Before the war the three main cereals occupied about equal places in the agricultural economy. Encouraged by the wheat subsidy, the wheat acreage rose to over 3,000,000 in 1943, but by 1949 oats accounted for a slightly larger acreage than either wheat or barley. The totals for that year show that oats occupied 1,946,271 acres in England and Wales, wheat 1,898,759 acres, and barley 1,884,844 acres. A comparison with the figures quoted on page 77 shows that while the wheat acreage has risen slightly a dramatic increase in the popularity of barley has been surpassed by a decline in that of oats.

Two main reasons are responsible for the change. First is undoubtedly the disappearance of the farm horse, for which oats were largely grown. The second is the relatively lower return per acre from oats than from barley, an important consideration as profits become tighter.

Nevertheless, in Scotland, Wales and northern and some western counties of England neither barley nor wheat offers a satisfactory alternative to oats, which are in those regions still widely grown. In northern counties they are often harvested unripe and fed in the sheaf to livestock. Alternatively they are threshed, the grain sold or home-mixed into a livestock ration and the straw also used as a feeding-stuff. In breeding oats, therefore, the plant-breeder has had to consider straw as well as grain.

Unlike wheat and barley, oats are probably indigenous to Britain. They may have derived from several wild species, though perhaps exclusively from *Avena sativa*, which itself is considered by some authorities to be the cultivated form of the wild oat, *Avena fatua*. Whatever their origins, they developed, during their prehistory, into innumerable local strains and races, almost every glen and parish having an oat claimed to be especially suitable to its soil and climate. Even now, with their diminished acreage, oat varieties are more numerous than those of either wheat or barley.

Dr John Garton, of Gartons Ltd, the Warrington firm, bred and introduced the first hybrid oat in 1892. This was the variety Abundance, which was followed in 1921 by another Garton-bred oat, Marvellous. Until after the war, however, most farmers continued to grow their local varieties; I remember that in the 1930s we had only Grey Winter oats for autumn sowing and Black Tartar for spring, often enough simply swopping seed with our neighbours.

In oats, as in other cereals, some of the most popular modern varieties have been introduced from Europe. Condor, for example, is a Dutch variety, Flamingskrøne a German one and Vigor a Belgian. We have in Britain, however, an unsurpassed plant-breeding station, engaged, though not exclusively, on breeding new varieties of oats. This, appropriately because of its climate, is the Welsh Plant Breeding Station at Aberystwyth. Founded in 1919, it devotes much of its energies to the breeding of grass varieties, but in cereals it specializes in oats, and from it many well-known varieties have emerged. The hall-mark of Aberystwyth is the letter 'S', used as a prefix for such internationally celebrated plants as S100 white clover and S24 rye-grass, and also occurring in several excellent varieties of oats, notably S147 and S172, though some of the Aberystwyth varieties now bear popular names, as, for instance, Manod.

Rye

Rye is thought to have been brought to England by the Anglo-Saxons and never achieved any great popularity. Essentially a crop of poor soils, it was usually grown where nothing else could be relied upon to give a satisfactory harvest. In 1963 the acreage was down to 17,000.

However, the past few years have seen a revived interest in rye for a different purpose. In the eastern counties of England it has long been the practice in spring to graze autumn-sown crops, chiefly wheat but also rye. Rye, being normally sown very early, as soon as the first harvest-fields are cleared, lends itself admirably to this treatment and, indeed, can often give an autumn grazing in November. Farmers having taken to sowing rye mainly for its grazing value, thus extending the grazing season at both ends, a demand arose for a rye specifically bred for the purpose. The role is filled at the moment by an excellent Polish rye known as Lovaszpatonai.

POTATOES

Of other crops than cereals from arable land the most important is potatoes, of which something over 500,000 acres are grown each year. The potato is one of America's contributions to our food supply. It was cultivated in South America long before that country was discovered by Europeans and was probably introduced into Spain early in the sixteenth century. Its introduction into England is generally ascribed to Sir Walter Raleigh in 1585 or 1586, but when Gerard, the herbalist, wrote in 1597 it was still an uncommon delicacy. The Royal Society appointed a committee to report on its potentialities in 1662, and by the end of that century it was being grown quite extensively in gardens. It was not until late in the eighteenth century, however, that, with the growth of a teeming urban population demanding cheap food, it began to be regarded as a farm crop. Transition to this status was most rapid in Ireland, where the population rose from 1,500,000 to 4,000,000 souls in the course of the eighteenth century. Having come to rely to a dangerous extent on a potato diet, the Irish were overwhelmed by an unprecedented disaster when the appearance of potato blight in 1845 and subsequent years caused the potato famine. Scotland was late in the field with potato cultivation, the first plot of potatoes being grown by one Thomas Prentice, in 1725.

Somewhat neglected as a field crop during the nineteenth century, the potato came into its own during the Second World War when farms were allotted compulsory quotas. By 1948 the acreage was over 1,000,000, producing over 8,000,000 tons of potatoes annually. Since then it has been gradually reduced and now stands at just over 500,000. Acreage and marketing are now regulated by the Potato Marketing Board, set up in 1934 and resuming operations after the hiatus of the war.

Throughout the years potatoes have become a specialized crop concentrated in districts eminently suited by climate and soil to their cultivation. The Fens, Lincolnshire, Lancashire, Lothian, Yorkshire and parts of Kent are examples of potato-growing districts, with Cornwall, Pembrokeshire and Ayr-shire specializing in earlies. During the past two decades, however, the prevalence of eelworm, through overcropping, has threatened the profitability of the crop in some of its old strongholds.

Target of a whole battery of diseases in this climate so dis-similar to that of its South American homeland, the potato has as some of its chief enemies a range of viruses, producing such phenomena as leaf roll, mosaic and stunted potatoes. It has now been established that these viruses are carried by aphides, which are less prevalent in the wet, cool climates of northern and north-western Britain than elsewhere. This is the explana-tion of the growth of the seed-potato industry in Scotland and, more recently, in Northern Ireland and the Isle of Man. Potato-growers go back year after year to these countries for certified virus-free stock.

SUGAR-BEET

The development of sugar-beet as a European crop began as Napoleon's answer to the British blockade around the year 1800. Cut off from their normal source of sugar supplies, the

West Indies, the French set about improving the sugar-beet plant, which grows in its wild state by the Mediterranean. The roots were thin, small, forked and tough, but contained up to 20% sugar. Louis de Vilmorin was the chief architect of the new brand of sugar-beet which, by the 1880s, had proved so successful that it was producing half the world's supply of sugar. None of it came from Britain, however. For experiments in British-grown sugar-beet we had to wait till 1909, and the first English factory was established at Cantley, Norfolk, in 1912 (and then largely with Dutch capital). Now there are seventeen factories, and the annual production of sugar-beet exceeds 5,000,000 tons.

PEAS

About 30,000 tons of peas are harvested in England each year for canning, drying and freezing, the industry being concentrated in Lincolnshire and adjacent counties. Their cultivation as a field crop is a recent development. Although garden peas were cultivated by the Romans, probably in Britain as elsewhere, they had apparently to be reintroduced in Tudor times and were reckoned a rather scarce delicacy in the reign of Queen Elizabeth I.

MARKET GARDENS

An unvarying phenomenon accompanying the growth of our great towns was the development of a market-garden belt around each. For London this zone in late Tudor times extended in a broad semicircle from Whitechapel through Islington to St James's and Hyde Park. R. S. R. Fitter, in *London's Natural History*, rightly asserts that by far the greater part of London is built on 'some of the richest market-garden land in England', inevitably so because market gardening has been an inescapable interim stage between the waste and the city. The horticultural fringe of London now, of course, lies much farther out, embracing the glasshouses of the

Lea Valley, the gardens of Kent and the flat market gardens of Middlesex.

Other cities and conurbations possess similar kitchen gardens. The Lancashire towns have the Ormskirk plain, the Midland cities have the Vale of Evesham, Bristol has the Bromham district of Wiltshire, and so on. In addition to these back gardens of industrial areas, which have sprung up on the nearest suitable soils, there are also areas of intensive cultivation which have only their soil and climate, and not the added advantage of proximity, to recommend them. Chief of these are Cornwall, the Channel Islands, Kent, the Hampshire coast, and the Fens. Of them the last-named is by far the most extensive.

After their reclamation, already mentioned, the Fens were farmed according to the standard pattern, growing grain and providing pasture for beasts. Indeed, until well on into the nineteenth century the Fenland pastures supported a huge livestock population and were reckoned to be among the best in England.

During the present century the potentiality of these rich soils, part alluvial, part peat and part clay, as producers of first-grade market-garden produce has been realized. Great depth, flatness and freedom from stones make them easily cultivable, while a high water-table, only a few feet below the surface, is ideally suited to the cultivation of certain crops, such as carrots and celery. Their development has been helped along by Dutchmen, who have recognized in the Fenland the counterpart of their own fertile polders, and nowadays the links between the Netherlands and the Fens are close, the same trading enterprises controlling farms in both countries in more than one instance. The whole zone, eighty miles from south to north and some ten to thirty miles in breadth, is now given over to intensive cultivation, its crops ranging from sugar-beet, potatoes, carrots, parsnips and cabbages to bulbs, flowers, celery, strawberries, and even such unusual items as carraway and dill. Although most of the crops are grown on a field scale, they are basically garden crops being given elbow-room. The history of each one runs along parallel lines. They were known in Roman times, survived the Dark Ages in monastery gardens, were reintroduced to the laity in the Tudor era, became popular in Stuart, Georgian and Victorian gardens, and have only latterly expanded to field stature.

Before turning to crops grown primarily or exclusively for animal fodder, however, we must glance at two or three anomalous ones.

Broad Beans

The broad bean has been cultivated on a field scale in Britain from time immemorial and until recent years very extensively. In the Midland and eastern counties in particular it provided much of the protein in home-mixed rations for livestock, particularly horses. Its acreage is now greatly diminished, but crops are still grown on the stiffer clay soils.

Hops

Although hops are native to England, they were not cultivated here until the sixteenth century. The practice of using hops in brewing was introduced from Italy in 1524, but was prohibited in the reign of James I, at the request of the City of London, as having a harmful effect on the beer! It is now one of the most rigidly controlled of all crops, its cultivation being confined to farms which for years have carried a 'hop quota', and marketing is entirely in the hands of the Hop Marketing Board. The acreage remains more or less constant at 20,000.

Flax

The occupation of Belgium and the Baltic lands by enemy forces in the Second World War necessitated attempts at growing flax, both for fibre and for oil, in Britain. By 1948 the acreage of flax for fibre in England and Wales alone had risen to over 85,000, with an additional 14,000 acres for linseed. As times reverted to normal, however, it was realized that our fields could not compete either in yields or in economic production with Continental growers. Consequently the flax crop has now shrunk almost to vanishing-point, not only in Britain but also in Northern Ireland, where it has traditionally occupied an important place in the economy and has been the foundation of the great Irish linen industry. A little flax is still grown for oil extraction.

Although we have at present no crop grown extensively for oil production, the emergence of a new one is always a possibility. At the University of Oxford's field laboratory at Wytham, near Oxford, Dr E. S. Bunting spends much of his time exploring the potentialities of likely plants. Opium poppies, rape seed, and safflower are among his subjects, and the two former are grown here and there in England on a field scale.

Leaving orchard fruit as being outside our province, though since the war blackcurrants have leaped into the role of a farm crop in many new districts, we turn now to crops grown specifically for livestock.

GRASSES

The revival of agriculture from 1939 onwards was due not only to the exigencies of war and the mechanization of farming processes but to the belated recognition of the importance of grass. Ours is one of the best climates in the world for growing grass (though, it may be added, one of the worst for conserving it). A magnificent collection of grasses clothes our countryside, from Cardigan to Kent and from Cornwall to Kincardine, with a luxuriant abundance of food for the grazing animal.

Its very prodigality led our ancestors for thousands of years to take it for granted. Grass was the natural cover for

the soil. You made use of what the good God provided and
were thankful.

Typical is the attitude of Thomas Davis of Longleat, whom
we find, when surveying Wiltshire farming for the Board of
Agriculture in 1810, praising to Heaven the 'Long Grass
Meads' of Orcheston. These were two tiny meadows, only
$2\frac{1}{2}$ acres together, lying along the course of a winterbourne
which for a few months of the year drains a section of Salisbury
Plain. After a wet spring these little fields, which were
apparently celebrated over much of southern England, produced a dense mat of herbage ideal for hay. Davis explains
that 'they depend entirely on floods; and being situated at a
sharp turn of a narrow part of the valley, the water makes an
eddy and deposits its sediment upon them'. Yet the grass was
only black bent, and, when I last saw it, some pretty poor,
coarse stuff, not to be compared with the rich leys on the
enveloping hills.

Davis was familiar with certain manures, such as ash, soot,
woollen waste and marl, but had evidently never thought of
applying them to grass. He notes that the Marquis of Bath
has used lime to improve grassland on poor gravelly soil near
Warminster, but did not think this was an example to be
followed elsewhere. The most you could do with permanent
grass was to get it a little earlier or a little lusher by irrigation, and mostly you left that to chance. He knew, too, of red
clover and rye-grass as one-year crops for hay, but between
such temporary stands and the great permanent pastures an
unbridgeable gulf was fixed.

Permanent pastures were, if anything, valued too highly.
They were almost sacred – to the extent, at any rate, of it
being near sacrilege to destroy one by the plough. Until the
Second World War most farm tenancies contained a clause
prohibiting a tenant from ploughing up an old pasture without
the landlord's permission, a permission often granted, if at all,
only on payment of heavy compensation. The proverb 'To
break a pasture makes a man; to make a pasture breaks a

man' was fully accepted. The general attitude to good pastures was exactly matched by the classic one of the old gardener who, on being asked by an American for the secret of his superb lawns, replied, 'We mows 'em for hundreds of years, and we rolls 'em for hundreds of years'. Even now there are still farmers and landowners who swear by the superior excellence of permanent pastures, and some tenancies still retain the old prohibition clauses.

In spite of this massive resistance to the idea of tampering with permanent pastures, the use of temporary grasses and clovers was slowly accepted. Red clover, cultivated by the Romans (though perhaps not in Britain), is reputed to have been reintroduced by Sir Richard Weston in the 1640s. Perennial rye-grass began to be grown as a seed crop about the same time, and sainfoin and lucerne are also seventeenth-century introductions. By the middle of the following century a seeds crop was an essential item in the Norfolk four-course rotation.

Red clover spread only very gradually to other parts of the country after becoming established in Norfolk, while sainfoin and lucerne were even slower in winning acceptance. Sainfoin eventually became a favourite crop on sheep farms in the chalk country, but lucerne lagged and has been introduced to many parts of Britain only within the past thirty years. In the eighteenth century experiments were made with several new species of herbage plants. Burnet proved more or less unsuccessful. Cocksfoot owed its first popularity to Coke of Holkham, who sent out the women and children of his estate to collect the ears at 3d. a bushel.

In the same century tentative experiments were made with sown permanent pastures, or long leys. In these mixtures white or Dutch clover was used as well as red, and other ingredients were trefoil, ribwort plantain and dwarf meadow grasses. A Norfolk farmer named Blomfield improved some of his pastures by pegging into them sections of selected turf and further augmenting the supply of the best varieties by sowing seeds thinly in spring.

Meantime the cultivation of rye-grass as a seed-producing crop developed as a speciality of certain districts, notably Northern Ireland.

It was the misadventures of perennial rye-grass that first inspired a detailed investigation into our wealth of indigenous grass species, leading to the ley-farming revolution.

The growers of this species for seed naturally valued the plants which gave the heaviest crop. Generations of such unconscious selection produced a type of rye-grass with much seed and stem but very little leaf. Consequently rye-grass acquired a reputation among farmers as being poor stuff. Yet when scientists began to examine our permanent pastures they found that perennial rye-grass was the commonest species and that here it was a leafy, short-stemmed plant. In the years just before the First World War scientists were starting to select some of the best leafy varieties of this rye-grass, which was now recognized as a very variable plant.

The Welsh Plant Breeding Station

After the war, in 1919, the Welsh Plant Breeding Station was established at Aberystwyth to investigate primarily grasses and leguminous plants. It had the remarkable good fortune to have appointed as its first Director Professor Sir R. George Stapledon, the father of modern ley farming.

Starting with a seven years' survey of the grasses of northern Cardiganshire, Stapledon made a thorough study of the material available. From Aberystwyth has emerged a series of remarkable grasses and clovers, their names prefixed by the letter 'S', which are the foundation of our modern leys. The natural tendency of all plants to veer towards the strains which produce the most seed is guarded against at Aberystwyth by the establishment of 'clone islands', which are isolated plots in which the original plant from which the strain was produced is preserved, thus enabling the scientists to return to the primary source whenever necessary.

WILD WHITE CLOVER

Although Dutch white clover was being used as an ingredient in experimental pastures in the eighteenth century, it was not until towards the end of the nineteenth century that the indigenous wild white clover was recognized as having even more to offer to the grazier. The plant is not only very persistent but the runners it sends out, under fertile conditions, help to bind the grasses together and so to create a good, turfy sward. The excellence of wild white clover was first appreciated as a result of experiments with basic slag on old pastures at Cockle Park, Northumberland, around the year 1906. There it was shown that when stimulated by basic slag the stock-raising capacity of wild white clover pastures was dramatically increased.

In the following two decades the demand for wild white clover seed increased enormously, as did its price. Nevertheless, the plant was not wholly satisfactory, being small and hence limited in yield. Once again, the Welsh Plant Breeding Station engaged in pioneering and produced that superlative hybrid, S 100 white clover, now familiar to farmers everywhere. Other valuable types have been developed in Kent and also overseas, notably the New Zealand Mother white clover.

AFTER THE PLOUGHING-UP CAMPAIGN

From the very beginning of the ploughing-up campaign of the Second World War it was realized that farmers were, in fact, cashing in on capital. They were exploiting the stored fertility of soil, accumulated during many years of quiescence. The proverb already quoted, 'To break a pasture makes a man; to make a pasture breaks a man', testified to the accepted profitability of the process. It was necessary, however, to look at the second and less attractive clause.

Here the twenty years of patient research by Professor Sir George Stapledon and his fellow scientists at last began to demonstrate their value. The pioneering Sir George preached the gospel that the new strains of grass and clover made the establishment of new pastures not only feasible but profitable. So during the 1940s the alternate husbandry or ley system of farming achieved popularity. It became recognized practice to sow a grazing or dual-purpose ley for a set period of years, generally from one to seven, and then to plough it under. During its career it was utilized as intensively as possible, by alternate mowings and grazings, the latter being controlled by electric fences, so that when the time came for it to be ploughed it had stored a valuable reserve of fertility. The time to plough a pasture is when it is looking its best, declared the ley-farming enthusiasts.

Their views have since been challenged. There is now a school of thought, of which Dr André Voisin, the Norman farmer-scientist, is a leading exponent, which maintains that permanent pastures are at least as productive as leys and much healthier. Doubt has been thrown on the wisdom of grazing animals on pastures consisting of only one or two species of plants. Such challenges are expected and salutary, yet, by and large, the ley system, with whatever modifications experience suggests, has proved itself sound and valuable and is now an accepted part of the British agricultural pattern.

The development of new methods of using and conserving grass will be dealt with in a later chapter. We now turn to other crops grown as stock feed.

TURNIPS

Turnips were well known to the Greeks and Romans, and their cultivation has probably continued on the Continent without a break. They were certainly grown extensively in Flanders in the fifteenth century and are said to have been introduced into England about 1550, though, as we have indicated previously, they may well have been grown here at a much earlier date. Gerard, writing in the reign of Queen

Elizabeth I, records that turnips were grown in the village of Hackney and sold by market-women at the Cross in Cheapside.

Sir Richard Weston, the advocate of red clover, was also championing the use of the turnip as a field crop in 1645, and in Stuart times it evidently had quite a following among farmers in the eastern counties. In 1701 Jethro Tull invented his seed-drill and his horse-hoe. Both were intended for use with cereals as well as with turnips, but both were certainly used with the latter crop. Indeed, Tull, at Prosperous Farm near Hungerford, intercropped autumn-sown wheat with turnips, pulling what roots survived in the spring. In general, the early cultivators of turnips allowed stock to eat them in the field rather than take the trouble to cart them to the farmyard. During Tull's lifetime Daniel Defoe reported that the East Anglian system of growing turnips for fattening sheep and cattle 'had spread over most of the east and south parts of England'.

The cultivation of turnips as a field crop was thus fairly well established before the era of Viscount Townshend, with whose name the turnip is everlastingly coupled. 'Turnip Townshend' he was nicknamed by those who were both amused and bored by this his sole topic of conversation.

> 'If a farmer "Turnip" cried
> On the day his father died,
> 'Twere no proof that he would rather
> Have a turnip than a father',

they chanted.

Nevertheless, his advocacy of the turnip as a field crop assisted English agriculture to take a great step forward. Whether he himself devised it or not, he certainly popularized the Norfolk four-course rotation, in which turnips were an integral part. The rotation is worth repeating.

Turnips; barley or oats; seeds (clover and rye-grass); wheat.

The role of the turnip was twofold. It provided valuable winter keep for animals which had formerly existed on the most meagre pickings; and, through the sheep being folded on the turnips in the field, it enriched the soil, to the extent that much land hitherto considered not worth cultivating could now produce corn crops. Later its value as a cleaning crop was also appreciated.

Although by the early nineteenth century the turnip was widely grown on these now traditional lines in most counties of southern and eastern England, it failed to achieve equal popularity in the Midlands and west. It also had, of necessity, to wait upon the passing of Enclosure Acts, its cultivation being virtually impossible under the old open-field system.

It remained the basis of sheep farming throughout most of arable England until the First World War, but declined with the sheep population in the 1920s and 1930s. Since then it has been superseded largely by the leafier brassica crops, such as kale, though considerable acreages are still grown.

SWEDES

The swede, or Swedish turnip, was introduced at some time during the second half of the eighteenth century. Both Arthur Young in Suffolk and Coke of Holkham in Norfolk thought highly of it and helped to popularize the crop. Coke evolved the method of stacking the topped roots in clamps and using them, sliced, as sheep food in severe weather. Their greater hardiness and higher dry-matter content have led to their maintaining their importance in the farming economy of the north and more particularly of Scotland.

MANGOLDS

Mangolds were likewise introduced towards the end of the eighteenth century, the actual year being, it is said, 1786. A novelty from France, they were at first cultivated for their leaves only, the roots being thrown away. The mangold took a long time to become established and was then confined chiefly to the south-eastern half of Britain. It is less hardy than the swede and than most varieties of turnip, though it gives a greater weight per acre (even though, as Professor Boutflour used to say, the weight is mostly of water). Its chief use was for cattle rather than sheep food, and it has been largely, though by no means entirely, superseded by kale and leys.

CABBAGES AND OTHER BRASSICAS

With cabbages we include kale, for they are simply two manifestations of the same plant.

Cabbage was a common vegetable in the ancient world and its cultivation in Britain probably never ceased, even in the Dark Ages. Whether it was used for stock food at all in the Middle Ages we do not know, the first reference to this being a suggestion by a writer, A. Speed, in 1659 that it could be so employed.

A hundred years later farmers were beginning to grow cabbages on a field scale, possibly in emulation of German farmers, who had been doing so for a long time. Arthur Young had a high opinion of its possibilities and records a number of examples of its value. He quotes, for instance, Simon Scroope, of Danby, Yorkshire, as growing cabbages averaging 13 lb. each, at a rate of $33\frac{3}{4}$ tons per acre, and a bumper crop of 54 tons per acre grown by a Mr Middlemore near Grantham. These were Scots cabbages, besides which Young lists six other varieties, 'the turnep, Battersea, Anjou, Russian, Red and Savoy'.

In 1767 a Mr Reynolds, of Addisham, Kent, introduced the kohlrabi as a field crop, for use as fodder in early spring. Its tops were eaten by cows and its roots dug out by pigs. It was, however, known as a garden crop at least as early as the sixteenth century.

Rape was grown in some parts of Britain from at least the

mid-eighteenth century onwards for the extraction of oil, but
its value for grazing must also have been realized. Thousand-
headed kale also has a fairly long but unrecorded career, but
marrow-stem kale is a more recent introduction, dating from
the end of the nineteenth century. It owes its rise in popularity to its value as a fodder crop for producing winter milk, a
product for which the demand increased greatly in the 1930s.

Fodder Beet

In the late 1940s and early 1950s several varieties of fodder
beet were introduced from Denmark, where they had been
evolved, as roots with a high dry-matter content for stock-
feeding, from sugar-beet types. It so happened that their British
sponsors had the wrong idea. They brought them in as a food
for pigs, which were still hampered by wartime rationing, and
the fodder beet proved not entirely satisfactory for the purpose. In Denmark I found the roots used predominantly for
feeding cattle.

Fodder beet is still listed by some merchants and is still
grown here and there, but it never achieved the hoped-for
popularity.

Maize

The development of maize as a silage crop has been similarly disappointing, though here the last chapter has by no
means been written.

Early in the nineteenth century some farmers, notably
William Cobbett, had hopes of it becoming a new grain crop,
as in America. These were nullified by our climate, in which
the varieties then known failed to ripen. Thereafter for more
than a century maize was treated as an auxiliary supply for
summer fodder, though, as it was cut from midsummer onwards, it had plenty of competitors and was not widely
cultivated.

In the late 1950s new varieties were introduced for use as a silage crop, the impetus being provided by the development of the forage-harvester, a machine which was able to deal with the huge, fibrous bulk offered by ripening maize. Instead of producing a generous growth of green matter at midsummer, these new varieties were required to grow cobs as near ripe as the British climate would allow. Harvesting could be postponed till October or even November, to give as long a ripening period as possible.

Most countries in the north temperate zone were at this time experimenting with maize varieties designed to push the maize belt northwards, and our N.I.A.B. tested over two hundred such varieties. A dozen or two proved useful for British conditions, and for a few years the acreage expanded rapidly. Heavy crops were grown (I myself took over 200 tons from 6 acres in 1960), and the cultivation techniques mastered. The resultant silage contained, on average, 20% to 25% dry matter, with protein content ranging from about 12% to over 20%. It was fed satisfactorily to dairy cows at rates of up to 60 lb. a day, though more commonly used only to provide part maintenance. Harper Adams College, which did a good deal of work with maize, found that bullocks eating about 80 lb. a day of maize silage, with the addition of 4 lb. a day of a protein supplement, made a weight gain of $2\frac{1}{2}$ lb. a day.

After these bright auguries, however, interest in the crop has waned. It was realized that, although the huge bulk of a mature maize crop was most impressive, its cost was about £30 an acre, and a farmer prepared to spend £30 an acre on a good grass-and-clover ley would probably get at least as heavy a yield in a succession of crops throughout the summer. Moreover, leys are less difficult to establish than a maize crop, which for the first six weeks of its life is very much at the mercy of weather, bird pests and weed competition (though thereafter it offers no complications).

Nevertheless, maize is still grown as a silage crop in many English counties and in a few in Scotland. Work proceeds, on an experimental farm in Essex and elsewhere, on evolving varieties which will yield a harvest of ripe cobs in our climate, and any year may see a revival of interest in the crop.

Lucerne and Other Leguminous Crops

Lucerne, trefoil, lupins and vetches were all grown by the Romans, though whether or not in Britain is not known. Both sainfoin and lucerne were introduced to English agriculture in the seventeenth century, but while sainfoin in due course established itself as a useful hay and grazing crop on chalk and limestone soils, lucerne lagged in popularity.

In the 1870s two German scientists, Hellriegel and Willfarth, established the relationship between leguminous plants and the nitrogen-assimilating bacteria which live in the nodules on their roots. Each species of leguminous plant has its own species of bacteria, normally found in the soil. Lucerne, being a plant of southern Europe, does not find its bacteria in English soils; hence its lack of success.

Once this was realized, it was a comparatively simple matter to inoculate lucerne seeds with the necessary bacteria, and all lucerne seed now sold is so treated. Since the practice became general lucerne has been more widely cultivated, being grown for grazing, hay, silage or grass meal. Its wonderful drought-resistance is not often tested in our climate, but its ability to produce a succession of heavy crops throughout the summer is highly valued. It is, however, a crop and slow to establish itself.

Trifolium, or crimson clover, is another southern plant so susceptible to frost that it can be grown only in southern England. It was introduced in the nineteenth century but has attained no great popularity.

Lupins of several varieties have been tried as a forage crop, but their chief though limited use in England is to provide a green manure crop on light, sandy soils in the eastern counties.

Vetches were in common use throughout the Middle Ages, certainly from Norse times onwards and maybe in the Saxon era. They may have remained in continuous cultivation from the Roman period. One assumes they were used chiefly as a green forage crop or for making hay.

6

THE STORY OF OUR LIVESTOCK

Cattle – Sheep – Pigs – Horses – Poultry and small game – Rabbits – The goat – The ass – The dog – The cat – Bees – New food for farm animals

CATTLE

WE have already noted the early origins of the two chief races of British cattle, the *Bos primigenius* and the *Bos longifrons*. We have seen, too, how difficult it is to trace the ancestry of any modern breed. For example, the occurrence of polled types of red cattle on either side of the North Sea and the higher incidence of these types in the eastern counties of Britain have suggested to many commentators that they were imported by the Danes and Norsemen in the eighth to tenth centuries. Yet we know that polled cattle lived in this country before the Roman era.

It is probable that each of the major invaders of Britain introduced at least some cattle, and a consideration of the purposes for which each of them used their animals will give clues to the type of beast brought in.

The Belgae introduced, in the last century before the Roman occupation, a heavy plough which seems to have been wheeled and to have turned a furrow. To draw it may have required the services of a four-ox or even an eight-ox team instead of the two oxen needed for the light *aratrum*. Did the Belgae bring over a stock of their own oxen from northern France, or did they make use of what they found here? Probably both. The imported animals would doubtless be heavy draught oxens descended from the aurochs and would thus increase our native stock of that type.

The likelihood is that the Romans found in this country a fairly adequate stock of heavy cattle, but a limited number of the lighter milking types. It has been conjectured that the Romans may have introduced milk cattle to Britain, the inhabitants formerly relying on sheep or goats for such milk as they used, but this seems unlikely. The Celtic *Bos longifrons* was so small and light that its primary use was probably for milk, and, in any event, it was from the Celts and Teutons of northern Europe that the Romans learned the art of buttermaking.

Nevertheless, the demand for butter, milk and cheese doubtless increased enormously with the advance of Roman civilization, and some cattle were almost certainly imported by the Romans. These would be animals of improved dairy type from the more advanced countries of the Mediterranean. Archaeology reveals, besides recognizable remains of cattle of both *Bos longifrons* and *Bos primigenius* types, two other sorts of cow, one resembling the modern Ayrshire and the other the modern Jersey or Guernsey. Tradition has it that the present wild white cattle of Britain were first introduced by the Romans, and this may be correct, for the predominant breeds of Italy and southern France in that era seem to have been white.

With the collapse of Roman civilization and the arrival of Saxon settlers we step back to a much more primitive type of agriculture. Whether the Saxons brought over their own cattle or used what they found on the land, it is probable that they employed them at first solely as draught animals, eating their meat when they were no longer fit for work. Milk and milk products seem to have been commodities of negligible importance in the early centuries of the Saxon occupation. On the other hand, milk, butter and cheese play quite a prominent part in the Welsh tradition.

We would thus expect to find Saxon England largely populated by mongrel races of heavy cattle bred for drawing the plough, while in the Celtic west the remnants of a wider range of more specialized types would find refuge. Here and there herds of escaped cattle would roam wild through the forests. And this, when light begins to illuminate again the agricultural scene, is what we do find. Nevertheless the situation is complex, for on the Bayeux tapestry we see among the booty being carried off by the Norman invaders a large white ox.

Early monastic records indicate that cattle were still being kept almost exclusively for draught purposes. This is true even of regions which later specialized in dairying, such as central Somerset, and butter and cheese were apparently made chiefly from the milk of sheep and goats. The development of the cow as a milk animal in England seems to date from about the thirteenth century, when we find the monkish record-keepers beginning to compare the milk yields of cows and sheep. About the same time horses were beginning to replace oxen as draught animals, so the cow had to find a new economic justification for its existence.

In the later Middle Ages cattle kept for all purposes were abundant. Their numbers fluctuated, however, with the exigencies of the climate and the incidence of sundry cattle diseases, all included in the ominous term 'murrain', which often took heavy toll. Hay and corn were the only provisions for winter use, and these were often in short supply. Oxen, needed for the spring cultivations, received priority. In autumn the numbers of stock were reduced, by slaughter, to a level which it was estimated could be maintained throughout the winter, but it is human nature to be optimistic, and many animals only just came through. Calving was normally confined to spring, though an autumn calver was considered an asset, and milk was therefore generally available only in summer. Considerable care was taken of cattle, however, the records containing details of their housing and grooming. The houses not only contained mangers, indicating stall feeding, but were in some instances heated in winter. Plough oxen were, according to one mediaeval chronicler, washed and curried twice a day.

Developments until the eighteenth century were slow. The chief concerned the demands of the growing towns for beef and dairy products. To supply these markets, and notably London, drovers began to bring herds and flocks from the distant parts of the kingdom. At the zenith of this great traffic enormous numbers of cattle and sheep travelled on the hoof, by well-established drovers' ways, from the Scottish Highlands, Wales, and the West Country, to the metropolis. In addition, fattening farms sprang up around London, to give these much-travelled beasts a better finish before they went to the butchers.

The specialist cheese-producing districts of England were already busy, notably Somerset, Cheshire, and Gloucestershire. Butter also was made in considerable quantities, but there was little trade in fresh milk. Both butter and cheese were, in the eighteenth century, being exported in quantities to the American colonies and arriving in good condition.

The animals producing these specialities were not, however, themselves specialized. They were expected to produce both meat and milk, and to draw a plough when necessary as well. In Tudor and Stuart times it is probable that cattle were imported to many parts of southern England and even Wales from the Netherlands, and there was doubtless a small cross-Channel trade with Normandy. No carefully planned and sustained effort seems to have been made, however, to achieve an improvement in either beef or milk production by an intelligent breeding programme.

Over the centuries, despite lack of deliberate purpose, definite types of cattle had emerged in the various provinces of the country and it may be useful, on the threshold of the great age of livestock improvement, to summarize what these were. Let us take a brief glance at the material on which the new cattle-breeders had to work.

Over most of the country cattle of the Longhorn type were dominant. This is natural enough when we remember that, although demands were changing, they were evolved from animals whose prime function was to pull a plough or a cart. Farmers now required their cattle to give milk in increasing quantities or to fatten more speedily, but they still used their traditional stock, the Longhorn. Though thus found in almost every corner of Britain, the Longhorn had its stronghold in the Midland shires.

The alternative early name for the Shorthorn, the Holderness, gives a clue to its origin. At the opening of the nineteenth century we find it concentrated there and in the adjacent parts of Yorkshire and Lincolnshire. It originated from imports of Dutch cattle to East Coast ports over a couple of centuries or so, crossed with the local cattle. Although primarily a red-and-white cow, with roan even then being particularly popular, there was no colour bar, and some of the early Shorthorns seem to have been black-and-white. In contrast to the Longhorn, the Shorthorn of the early eighteenth century was already reckoned a dairy breed, and as the century progressed attempts were made to improve its milking qualities by crossing with imported Channel Island bulls.

Having thus sorted out their Longhorns and Shorthorns, our agricultural ancestors now lumped a whole range of types together as 'middlehorns'. Prominent among these were the red cattle of Devon, Sussex, and Hereford, progenitors of the breeds which now bear those names.

The red Devons seem to have been established in their county from very early times, and by the end of the seventeenth century were already earning a reputation as good beef animals. Both Sussex and Herefords were reckoned by some eighteenth-century writers to be simply local varieties of Devons, and almost certainly they had a common ancestry, even if there was no direct reinforcement by crossing one with another. It is likely that the Hereford owes some characteristics, perhaps its white face, to importations of Dutch cattle. A similar white-faced type of red cattle was also found at this period in Norfolk; it, too, doubtless owed something to Dutch importations, though the emphasis was entirely on beef, it being a quick-maturing, fleshy breed with no milking qualities.

In Gloucestershire, Somerset, and north-west Wiltshire, and also farther west in the Vale of Glamorgan, the predominant type was a fine-boned, milk-producing cow of a deep red or brown colour with a white stripe, or finching, along the spine and tail. A few of these Old Gloucestershire cattle still survive, though vigorous efforts may have to be made soon if the breed is to be saved from extinction. Their prime asset was milk rich in large globules of butterfat from which the celebrated Double Gloucester cheeses were made. In the eighteenth century they were already being superseded by Longhorn cattle, then more prolific in milk yields, spreading down from the north.

Central Somerset also had a 'sheeted' cow, which somewhat resembled the Belted Galloway, except that the whole of its rear half was white. It appears to have been a beef type.

Whether the South Devon breed was then in existence is not known. Probably it was, though perhaps not in so distinctive a form as the present specimens. Its origin seems to have been in crosses between the native red Devons and cattle imported from the Channel Islands and Normandy, though some of the imports may have come from farther south in France and have been of the ancestors of the Charolais. A distinct resemblance exists between the South Devon and many of the modern Charolais crosses.

Moving eastwards along the Channel coast, most of the local cattle probably owed much to importations from the Channel Islands and France. Within living memory the distinctive brindled cattle which still graze, though in greatly diminished numbers, in the New Forest, were said to derive their colouring from 'Isigny' bulls from Normandy.

Cattle from the Channel Islands were formerly grouped under the common name of 'Alderney'. As the eighteenth century advanced and milk-producing qualities became more highly valued, a growing demand for Alderneys arose from many parts of the country, even from as far afield as Scotland

and Ireland. The fallacy that, because of their more feminine build, they were delicate was slowly dispelled.

While along the southern coast, such as the New Forest, the Isle of Wight, and the Exeter district, Alderney blood predominated, in Kent it was superseded by the contribution of imported Dutch cattle, many of which came in during the seventeenth century. Crossed with mongrel local cattle, largely of Sussex type, these produced a sort of cattle known as Kentish Home-bred which were fattened in large numbers for the London market.

North of the Thames, in Suffolk, a polled cow known as the Suffolk Dun had a high reputation as a milk-producer. It was, of all the types we have been considering, the one most like a modern beef animal, being small, quick to fatten and producing a large carcass on short legs. Undoubtedly it was one of the chief ancestors of the modern Red Poll, but at this time its colour was variable, ranging from red to dun or greyish-yellow.

This is the first polled type we have met, but there were others. On the eastern slopes of the Pennines, in certain Yorkshire and Derbyshire dales, lived a polled variety of Shorthorn capable of high milk production.

Farther north, in Scotland, polled cattle were common. The ancestors of the modern Galloway occupied much of the territory south of the Highland Line and formed a good proportion of the drovers' herds trotting southwards to provide London with roast beef. Indeed, it seems that the preference of the drovers for polled rather than horned cattle, for obvious reasons, led to the development of the polled strain, for originally the Galloways were both of polled and horned types. Their colour was variable.

The original Angus had nothing very distinctive about them, apart from their relatively small size. Of mongrel ancestry and scattered over the counties of Aberdeen and Angus, they were of black, dun or brindled colour and might be either polled or horned. Before the nineteenth century they counted for little.

Beyond the Highland Line roamed the Highland cattle or Kyloes. They seem to have differed little from the modern representatives of the breed, though were perhaps a trifle smaller.

Polled cattle were also found locally in parts of Sutherland and the Isle of Skye, and in Shetland and Orkney lived the dwarf Shetland cattle which still survive in diminished numbers.

The Aryshire breed is said to have originated in the parish of Dunlop in the seventeenth century and were alternatively known as Dunlops. They were apparently based on a type of cattle, once common in lowland Scotland, which resembled the English Longhorn and had the characteristic white finching, though some writers have held them to be quite distinct from this indigenous breed and to have been developed from crosses between Dutch and Alderney cattle, with an admixture of Shorthorn blood from the Tees valley. Probably cattle of all these types played their part in the development of the breed, which was evolved with the deliberate intention of producing a fine milk cow capable of thriving on the wet Ayrshire pastures.

Over on the other side of Scotland, Fifeshire was the home of another variety of milk, or rather dual-purpose, cattle. These were large black cows with upturned horns, like the modern Ayrshire. Their ancestry is unknown, and they are now extinct.

In Wales from very early times black cattle have been dominant. At the end of the seventeenth century the purest (if such a word can be used in this context) aboriginal stock was found in the mountains of Merioneth and neighbouring counties, where it had bred almost untouched by improvement or by the introduction of outside blood from time immemorial. In the lowland fringes of the country, notably in the south, the old Welsh blacks had been altered by contact with English breeds, and there had been an influx of Dutch cattle into Pembrokeshire. Many of these southern cattle resembled the

Old Gloucestershires and because of their superiority were gradually moving up into the Welsh highlands.

Along the Welsh/English border the blacks were replaced by a red or brown breed, no doubt one of the ancestors of the modern Hereford, though most of the cattle seem to have had smoky rather than white faces.

Here and there in Wales pockets of white cattle were apparently to be found, while another evidence of the forcing of the old Celtic types westwards was to be found in the remnants of a small, black breed of cattle, like the modern Kerry, in that other Celtic peninsula, Cornwall.

With the development of the drovers' trade, however, the flow changed direction. The Welsh cattle came cascading back into England. Primarily, of course, they were butchers' animals bound for the London market, but many of them found their way to fattening pastures from Leicestershire to Romney Marsh, and no doubt some were incorporated into breeding herds.

Such was the basic stock on which the great livestock breeders of the eighteenth and early nineteenth centuries had to work, and we are now about to see them in action.

We must be aware that already many farmers appreciated the need to improve their cattle and had taken steps to do so. On the whole, however, their activities had amounted to little more than the introduction of alien blood in somewhat vague attempts to effect a general improvement. The innovation of Bakewell and his contemporaries and successors was to select certain desirable characteristics and to plan a breeding programme to establish them.

Unfortunately for some of the existing types of cattle these early improvers had one motive, to breed a well-fleshed, quick-maturing beef animal for the London market. In following this objective they sacrificed the milking qualities of some of the older breeds.

Many of the details of Robert Bakewell's career are obscure. The son of a farmer, he was born in 1725 and worked

with his father till 1760, when he took over the sole management of the ancestral farm, at Dishley, in Leicestershire. He
died in 1795, it is said in poverty, having become bankrupt,
although he seems to have been able to bequeath the Dishley
inheritance intact to his nephew.

His claim to fame lies in his work for the improvement of
his cattle and sheep, in pursuit of which he employed a novel
but scientifically correct principle. Instead of seeking to effect
improvement by introducing attractive animals of other
breeds or from other distincts, Bakewell concentrated on in-
breeding, reinforced by rigid selection and culling to bring
out the characteristics he wanted. With sheep he was out-
standingly successful; with cattle, less so, largely because the
breed he chose, the Longhorn, had a limited capacity for the
improvements he had in mind.

Such is the generally accepted version of Bakewell's life and
work, but, as often happens when a new idea is pioneered,
there were others who shared the work if not the limelight.
Bakewell did not conceive the idea of in-breeding in a vacuum;
the principle was well known to racehorse-breeders. It seems,
too, that he was not the first to apply it to cattle. In the village
of Canley, near Coventry (which is sufficiently near Dishley
for Bakewell to have known what was going on), a Mr
Webster was building up a herd of formidable local reputation, when Bakewell was a youth, by similar or identical
methods. Both Bakewell and his chief fellow experimenter,
Robert Fowler of Rollright, drew heavily on the Canley stock
for their herds.

Publicity came to Bakewell through Arthur Young, one of
the earliest and most effective of agricultural propagandists,
who visited him at Dishley in 1770. A word about the career
of this remarkable man, to whom we owe much of our information about events and personalities of this important period
in the history of farming. The son of a Rector of Bradfield,
near Bury St Edmunds, Young was born in 1741. From 1763
to 1771 he farmed first at Bradfield and then in Essex, con-

stantly experimenting, usually without success, and eventually being forced out of both farms. An indefatigable traveller, he published, beginning in 1768, a series of books describing his agricultural tours, first in England and then in Ireland and France. His analytical mind and penetrating observation drew attention to agriculture as a genuine science and prepared the way for the flood of future progress. Appointed secretary to the Board of Agriculture in 1793, he initiated surveys into the state of agriculture in eight English counties, and also continued his own voluminous writings. His *Farmer's Kalendar* eventually ran through over 200 editions. He died, blind, in 1820.

What Bakewell attempted to do for the Longhorn, Robert and Charles Colling now did more successfully with the Shorthorn. These brothers, who farmed at Ketton and Brampton, near Darlington in County Durham, were pupils of Robert Bakewell. In 1784 they acquired a bull, *Hubback*, on which, by in-breeding and selection, they founded the improved Shorthorn breed. *Hubback* himself had no distinguished ancestry. On one side he was not far removed from imported Dutch stock, on the other he was nearly related to Highland cattle. Nevertheless he had qualities which the Collings were shrewd enough to appreciate, and, what was more important, he was able to transmit them consistently to his offspring. The extent of the in-breeding practised is illustrated by the pedigree of the bull *Comet*, sold for the unprecedented sum of a thousand guineas. *Comet* was the progeny of a bull on his own daughter; this sire's dam was the progeny of a bull on her own mother; and the sire was the progeny of near brother and sister.

Like Bakewell, the Collings directed their efforts to producing beef animals, with the graziers and the London market in mind. At one stage they deliberately introduced red Galloway blood into their Shorthorn herd. They were also, in spite of their selection of quick-growing, well-proportioned stock, still half in love with the older conception of huge, grossly fat beef beasts. It was Charles Colling who bred the celebrated, or notorious, Durham Ox, which spent six years touring Britain and displaying to fascinated audiences its 27 cwt. of flesh and bone.

In the pursuit of an efficient beef animal much milk had been lost. Here it will be instructive to pause for a moment and note just how productive some cows had been on the threshold of the age of improvement.

Robert Trow-Smith estimates 'a figure of about 500 gallons a year in a well-managed Longhorn herd in Wiltshire'. Arthur Young, in his *A Tour in Ireland*, records a crossbred Longhorn/Shorthorn herd at Mallow some members of which gave up to 12 gallons a day, with thrice-daily milking. Of Shorthorns, Young gives numerous instances of yields of from 5 to 9 gallons a day, and one, of a cow belonging to a Mr Whittam, of Rothbury, Northumberland, of a yield of 24 gallons a day! Shorthorn milk was, however, notoriously low in fats and therefore little valued for cheese-making. A polled strain of Shorthorns found in Yorkshire and Derbyshire were capable of giving 5 or 6 gallons a day, while the Suffolk Dun, reckoned to be one of the best English milkers, commonly gave 6 and often 8 gallons a day. The extinct Fifeshire breed gave 5 to 7 gallons a day for the early months of lactation, while the Ayrshire yielded 5 gallons a day of milk very rich in fats.

Even types which later developed into pure beef breeds were by no means negligible milkers. In Dorset, Arthur Young saw a Devon cow which gave $6\frac{1}{4}$ gallons a day, and the nearly-related Sussex could be coaxed up to 4 gallons. Certain strains of the Galloway were said (by Colonel Fullarton, who wrote in 1793) to give 'great quantities of milk'.

Evidently the best milkers of the early eighteenth century were not much inferior to good modern dairy cows.

As the first improvers were interested in beef alone (and as they probably did not realize, in any case, that the beef qualities they were achieving were not compatible with milk production), milking qualities tended to slip and had to be retrieved. One of the first dairy champions in the field was

Thomas Bates, of Kirklevington, in Yorkshire. Born in 1775, and hence a younger contemporary of Bakewell and Collings, he farmed at Kirklevington from 1830 to 1849, during which time he built up the Kirklevington herd which was the foundation of the modern Dairy Shorthorn breed and to which most Dairy Shorthorns can trace their ancestry. Bates did not, however, pursue milking qualities to the exclusion of all others with the single-mindedness of the beef-breeders. Using their improved stock he attempted to breed back some milk into it without altering its good, beefy looks. The result was the compromise which has handicapped the Dairy Shorthorn ever since.

Following the path pioneered by Bakewell, the Collings and their contemporaries, breeders now began to take other indigenous stock in hand. We will briefly sketch the story of the development of the modern breeds.

THE LONGHORN

Bakewell's efforts to produce a quick-maturing beef animal were unsuccessful. The Longhorn took too long to grow and was superseded by brisker new breeds. From its position of supremacy its numbers dwindled until now it is represented by a few hundred cattle on Midland pastures.

THE SHORTHORN

We have already noted how from the earliest period of improvement the Shorthorns developed along two lines, the beef and dairy types.

Among the purchasers of Collings' stock were several Scottish farmers who, for the next thirty or forty years, quietly bred a purely beef type, with precious little regard for milking qualities. These Beef Shorthorns later returned to England and also superseded the Longhorns in Ireland. Even later they proved the ideal stock for many of the new countries overseas.

Meantime the Dairy Shorthorn, becoming with the failure of the Longhorn almost supreme in many parts of England, was wasting its opportunities by developing fine show points rather than concentrating on milk production. It was this preoccupation with the show ring rather than performance which eventually gave the Friesian its chance.

Probably not as a deliberate protest against this trend or against the development of the Beef Shorthorn, but certainly as an attempt to salvage the excellent milking qualities inherent in the original Shorthorn stock, farmers in the four northern counties of England developed a milking strain which is now recognized as the Northern Dairy Shorthorn breed. This lighter, long-legged version of the Shorthorn specializes in milk production.

The Lincoln Red Shorthorn originated in the first age of improvers with the whim of one Thomas Turnhill, of Beasley, in Lincolnshire, to have a herd of entirely deep-red cattle. As he could draw from some of the best Shorthorn stock on their home pastures, he was able to start an excellent breed which has become predominant in Lincolnshire and has spread to many other counties. At first it was dual-purpose; then it developed both dairy and beef strains separately; and now the beef strain has become dominant, with very few dairy herds surviving. A polled strain has been developed in recent years, and the breed has been moving into Scotland and to countries overseas.

THE DEVON

Towards the end of the eighteenth century, when it became the fashion to experiment with various types of cattle, Devons were taken from their native pastures to a number of farms in the North and Midlands. The most notable export was to Thomas Coke's farm at Holkham in Norfolk, where a large herd became one of the sights of the farm. Coke's enthusiasm did much to popularize the breed.

Meantime in Devon a far-sighted breeder, Francis Quartly, of Molland, near South Molton, gathered the control of the emerging Devon breed into his own hands. During the Napoleonic Wars, when most breeders were cashing in on the high prices and disposing of their stock, Quartly rescued the best cattle he could find and laid the foundations of an extremely fine herd, from which most modern Devons are descended.

The Hereford

The Hereford had the advantage of expanding in a vacuum, or, rather, of supplanting the casily ousted Longhorns in the west Midlands. Its early improvers divided into two groups, one concentrating on colour (notably the white face) and the other on conformation regardless of colour. By the 1840s the white face had been combined with the conformation to create the Hereford type which has thenceforth never varied. From the 1870s onwards great numbers were exported to America and other new countries.

The Sussex

Until comparatively recent years the Sussex, third of the red breeds, was little affected by the improvers. These heavy red cattle continued in their immemorial role of hauling ploughs through the stiff clay soils of the Weald, their surplus stores being turned to beef. Since the Second World War the Sussex has made considerable efforts to improve its beef performance and can be reckoned among our leading beef breeds. It has provided much stock for South Africa.

The Galloway

This is another breed left virtually untouched by the eighteenth- and nineteenth-century improvers. No doubt it was taken in hand by individual farmers, and somewhere along the line it lost its dual-purpose qualities and became purely a beef breed, but there was no large-scale and persistent attempt, as with many other breeds, to develop it. Consequently it remained, until very recently, a slow-maturing but very hardy beef breed, confined more or less to its native hills in south-west Scotland. Recently, and particularly since the Second World War, it has been making up for lost time. It has refined its craggy frame, speeded up its growth rate and has spread far from its native moors, even to the Home Counties of England, where it is, perhaps unfortunately, popular as an ornamental adjunct to millionaires' estates.

THE ABERDEEN-ANGUS

As we have seen, the progenitors of the Angus breed were in the early eighteenth century the black but mongrel dual-purpose cattle inhabiting the north-eastern counties of Scotland. Until the 1830s little progress was made, but the breed was then taken in hand by certain efficient and enterprising breeders. Its two chief pioneers were Hugh Watson, of Keiller, in Angus, and William McCombie, of Tillyfour, in Aberdeenshire. McCombie in particular put in such excellent work for twenty or thirty years from 1857 onwards that the improved Aberdeen-Angus forged far ahead of any of its competitors, except its chief rival, the Beef Shorthorn. It was in 1857 that he first hit the headlines by taking six of his almost unknown, home-bred cattle to the Paris International Livestock Exposition and winning with them four prizes, including two firsts. With its small, quick-maturing carcass of prime beef the Aberdeen-Angus was just in time to play a major part in populating the New World with beef herds.

THE HIGHLAND

The chief asset of this breed being its ability to thrive on the bleak, wet hills of the Highlands and the Hebrides, the

Highlanders could never have been material for the sort of improvement attempted on Lowland breeds. Nevertheless the great landlords of the mountains have for the past hundred and fifty years exercised a wise control over the development of the breed and have improved its performance as far as was possible without jeopardizing its hardiness.

THE WELSH BLACK

This other breed of the Celtic hills remains now comparatively unimproved. All the divergent types were gathered together in one herd book in 1874, but even now there are beef strains and dairy strains, and in the mountains of Merioneth a useful polled strain exists. One thing the Welsh Blacks have always lacked is a good publicist. Most breeders are small farmers who do not normally exhibit at shows and are reasonably content with their present dual-purpose animal. Recently the breed has attracted more outside interest, and herds have moved out of Wales into lowland England, repeating a former migration of the days when they were a favourite drovers' beast for the London market.

THE SOUTH DEVON

This excellent breed, which we saw established from unknown antecedents in the district of south Devon known as the South Hams, has remained there, apart from colonizing parts of east Cornwall. It seems to have everything, including a huge carcass (it is the largest British breed), good milking capacity, and milk of high quality, of the same category as Channel Island milk. Recent tests have illustrated its ability to put on weight quickly and produce the lean meat now demanded. Nevertheless it is little known outside its native corner, largely, I think, because its numbers are so small and its breeders so contented that any demand for stock which does arise cannot usually be met.

THE RED POLL

This is the breed that arose as the result of an amalgam between those two ancient East Anglian types, the Norfolk Red and the Suffolk Dun. It was being slowly developed throughout the first half of the nineteenth century, and the breed society dates from 1888. Both the parent breeds have since become extinct. It is a useful dual-purpose breed but is making efforts to improve its performance in both directions.

THE AYRSHIRE

Turning to the purely dairy breeds, the Ayrshire came early into the field as a productive milker living on the doorsteps of Glasgow and Edinburgh. Colonel Fullarton, mentioned above and writing in 1794, stated that for more than a century the cattle of the Cunningham district in northern Ayrshire had been noted for milk, and the cattle he describes were, apart from the absence of the distinctive upsweeping horns, very similar to modern Ayrshires. The beginning of the evolution of the Ayrshire as a distinct breed can thus be pushed farther back in history than that of most breeds, but even so its ancestry is doubtful. Imports of Dutch cattle, either direct from Holland or via England, played some part in its inheritance, as did probably the English Shorthorn. The contention that the breed contains Channel Island blood is more doubtful, but several indigenous Scottish types are certainly represented.

Whatever its antecedents the Ayrshire was soundly established as a specialist milk-producer early in the nineteenth century, when nearly every other breed or type was trying for dual-purpose laurels. W. Youatt, writing in 1834, recorded that a good average for an Ayrshire was 900 gallons a year. Before that date Ayrshires were being exported to Canada and U.S.A. for dairy herds, and before the middle of the century a trade had developed with Sweden and Finland as well. The breed was also in demand in many parts of England, and in the present century its popularity received a new impetus through being able to offer, in the early days of the campaign for the eradication of bovine tuberculosis, a very large selection of attested dairy animals.

The Guernsey

Early writers do not always, or indeed often, differentiate between the Guernsey and the Jersey, referring to Channel Island cattle indiscriminately as 'Alderneys'. Both islands were inhabited, in the seventeenth century and earlier, by types of cattle similar to those on the adjacent mainland of France. Originally the cattle were triple-purpose, with the task of pulling a plough doubtless their prime function, but by the early eighteenth century they were already achieving a reputation in England for milk-production. Shipments across the Channel attained such proportions that soon after the end of the Napoleonic Wars the island stock had become scarce. In Guernsey at least some Shorthorns were then imported to increase supplies and also to build up the size and conformation of the breed, until the traffic was prohibited. Since then it has been impossible to import any sort of cow into the islands, even Guernseys sent to Britain for show purposes being permanently banished.

The Jersey

Mr Eric Boston, the biographer of the Jersey breed, thinks we should look for its origins in the East, and he points out its similarity to animals depicted in Egyptian tombs. It is also his opinion that most of the domestic cattle of north-western Europe were brought from the East rather than tamed from indigenous wild stock. In his book *Jersey Cattle* he traces in some detail the possible contributions made to the breed by the several ancient types of cattle found in neighbouring countries, not forgetting the Dutch, which seem to have found their way to the Channel Islands as well as to Britain in some numbers in the seventeenth and eighteenth centuries. The first legal prohibition of the import of cattle to Jersey (though it was a fiscal measure rather than an attempt to preserve the purity of the race) was made in 1763, since when restrictions have been tightened up, as in Guernsey.

The impulse to improve the breed and to establish a breed society came from England. In 1811 a Mr Michael Fowler, who was a partner in a company owning a dairy in Hyde Park, bought for £7 a Jersey cow at Barnet Fair. Its diminutive size suggested to him that it would be a suitable present, though of no great utilitarian value, for his wife. He was amazed when the little cow produced 14¼ lb. of butter weekly for the first seventeen weeks after calving. On enquiry he found that the cow had come over with a small consignment to Southampton, and he quickly set about making contacts with breeders in Jersey and establishing a regular import trade. Later, on visits to Jersey, he informed the breeders of developments in cattle-breeding and of the organization of agricultural societies and shows which were then taking place in England. A direct result was the formation of the Royal Jersey Agricultural Society in 1833, with the establishment of a herd book five years later.

It is interesting to note that, although small numbers of Jerseys were finding their way to South Coast ports in 1811, the cattle were unusual enough to be a complete novelty to this experienced London dairyman (and also to most of his contemporaries, for the story has it that the vendor of the cow failed to find a buyer at Barnet Fair and sold it to Fowler at a bargain price on the way home).

The Jersey has now found its way to most cattle-keeping countries, being strongly represented in U.S.A., Canada, Australia, South Africa, France, and Denmark, and comprising more than 80% of the cattle of New Zealand.

The Friesian

We have already noted the imports of 'Dutch' cattle to many parts of Britain and their role in the improvement of a number of our breeds. Their origins in their native country are as obscure as those of cattle breeds anywhere. In the late Middle Ages the Netherlands seem to have been a half-way house for a very considerable traffic in cattle. Great numbers of cattle were brought annually from Denmark and northern Germany to be fattened on Dutch pastures and then passed on to Spain and Portugal. The general Dutch or Friesian type seems to have been established not earlier than the second half of the eighteenth century, and J. K. Stanford, the biographer of the breed, in his book *British Friesians*, mentions that it was not until after 1800 that great attention was paid to cattle-breeding. Both black-and-white and red-and-white were recognized colours, as they still are in Holland (which now has four breeds). From 1820 to 1850 the ravages of cattle disease so depleted the Dutch herds that they were reinforced by imports of English Shorthorns, an episode occasionally brought to mind by the occurrence of a roan animal in pied Dutch herds. It was in the second half of the nineteenth century that the present Dutch breeds became finally fixed.

Although cattle from Holland had been entering East Coast ports for centuries it was not until 1909 that the British Friesian Cattle Society was formed. With the improvement in Dutch stock in their home country very large numbers were sent over (over 351,000 between 1872 and 1877, for example), primarily for slaughter. Fear of disease caused this trade to be prohibited in 1892, but by that time a nucleus of breeding herds had been established in the eastern counties. After the formation of the Society animals were admitted on inspection till 1913, since when entry has been by pedigree only. The breed has subsequently been reinforced by five importations – one from Holland in 1914, one from South Africa in 1922, one from Holland in 1936 (with the aim of improving the butterfat content of the milk), one from Canada in 1946, and one from Holland in 1950.

In a little over forty years the breed has swept the country, largely superseding the native though usually non-pedigree Dairy Shorthorn and becoming the predominant dairy breed. Within the last decade it has also come to the front as a beef breed, eminently suitable for producing quick-maturing, lean beef in mass-production beef feedlots.

RED-AND-WHITE FRIESIAN

Although black-and-white is the only colour officially permitted by the rules of the British Friesian Cattle Society, red-and-white was an original Friesian colour, and red-and-white throwbacks occur from time to time in pedigree herds. In recent years certain breeders who have objected to the rigid insistence on black-and-whites have collected the rejected red-and-whites into a number of herds for which they have now formed a herd book and breed society. Although theoretically colour is the only difference, the red-and-whites I have seen seem to be more beefy animals.

THE BRITISH–CANADIAN HOLSTEIN–FRIESIAN

This is another offshoot of the British Friesian. Between the two world wars, and subsequently in the late 1940s, numbers of Canadian Friesians were brought into Liverpool and other west coast ports. They tend to be rather smaller than our home-bred Friesians but produce large quantities of milk of relatively high butterfat content. As the British Friesian Cattle Society would not recognize or accept into its herd book any of these Canadian imports, other than those from its official importation in 1946, the breeders who had acquired them formed their own breed association.

THE KERRY

Although this breed does not nowadays amount to much in

British livestock economy it is one of the most venerable of all British types, being the direct descendant of the ancient black Celtic cattle once so numerous in Britain. The breed takes its name from the mountainous county of Kerry, its chief remaining stronghold, but it was probably once dominant in Ireland. In England it has become established chiefly as a house cow on rural estates. Like the Guernsey and Jersey it is small and dainty and looks well in a park background. Its claim is economic milk production, 'not less than 100 gallons of milk per cwt. of cow', and it maintains its position without making much headway.

THE DEXTER

The Dexter is derived from the Kerry, or rather from the black Irish cattle from which the modern Kerry has descended. It owes its distinctive type primarily to a Mr Dexter who endeavoured, after the fashion of the times, to improve the beef qualities of the Irish blacks in the late eighteenth century. The breed was introduced into England in 1882, since when its history has roughly paralleled that of the Kerry, having earned its place as a park and house cow.

It is now dual-purpose, is very economical to feed and produces milk of a high butterfat content. An outstanding feature of the breed is its short legs, and these are associated genetically with dwarf characteristics which also produce occasional monstrosities, such as bulldog-headed calves.

SHEEP

We have briefly mentioned the probable derivation of our domestic breeds of sheep from two wild species, the mouflon and the urial, and have drawn attention to the very primitive type still surviving on St Kilda. Archaeologists testify that although sheep were introduced to this country by Neolithic man their remains do not become numerous till the Bronze Age. This increase seems to have coincided with the introduction of the art of weaving wool.

We have also noted a trend towards large-scale sheep-farming in late Roman times. British woollen cloth was known in Rome, and it is likely that the southern half of our country sustained a very large sheep population.

Evidence for this period and for the following five or six hundred years is, however, very meagre, and the Domesday Book (compiled in 1086) gives us our first real glimpse of sheep in the rural economy. Sheep-farming in Saxon and mediaeval England has been dealt with in a masterly essay by W. G. Hoskins in his recent book *Provincial England*. He states that the number of sheep listed in the eight counties (four in East Anglia and four in the south-west) for which figures are given in Domesday is roughly 300,000. These statistics are for demesne lands only (i.e. lands owned by manorial lords), and surveys made a little later indicate that the amount of stock owned by the peasantry was about four times as great, though more in some instances, such as on the Glastonbury estates. From these facts he deduces that the number of sheep on demesne lands in the forty counties of England at the end of the eleventh century may have been about 1,500,000, and those on the peasant holdings a further 6,000,000, making a total of 7,500,000. For comparison the present total for England and Wales is just short of 20,000,000.

Hoskins concludes that not only was the wool trade of England thoroughly established at least as early as the tenth century but that it was well distributed throughout the kingdom; and also that, while the great abbeys and estates played an important and fairly well-publicized part in the trade, the contribution of the peasant farmer with his small flocks was probably more important.

In an earlier chapter we have given an account of the mediaeval wool trade and of methods of managing the flock. Compared with cattle and other domestic livestock there is such a wealth of documentary references to sheep as to be embarrassing. Innumerable records of abbey and lay estates and the trading accounts of merchants and shipping agents are all filled with details of sheep and wool.

In spite of the ever-recurrent 'murrain' of the Middle Ages and the economic changes of Tudor and Stuart times, the sheep population continued to increase until at the beginning of the eighteenth century, when, as with cattle, we enter the age of improvers, it probably stood at about 12,000,000.

Modern sheep breeds, of which we have over forty in Britain – by far the greatest number of any country in the world, – are divided into four classes: (*a*) long-woolled, (*b*) short-woolled, (*c*) hill, and (*d*) mountain and moorland. The well-known down breeds are included among the short-wools. Prototypes of all these existed in the year 1700, as we shall discover when we examine their origins. We will make this survey geographically, starting in the south-eastern corner of England.

The Kent, or Romney Marsh

The superb grazing of Romney Marsh has encouraged the large-scale keeping of sheep from time immemorial. It was almost certainly well populated by sheep in Roman days, and the large animals referred to in mediaeval documents may well have descended from Roman stock. The breed was improved by the judicious introduction of blood from the new Leicester breed (see below) between 1810 and 1820, which improved its performance without detracting from its hardiness.

The Romney Marsh, a long-woolled breed, has a most impressive export record. By far the greater proportion of sheep in New Zealand belong to it, while vast numbers flourish in Australia, Argentina, Chile, Uruguay, Peru, Brazil, U.S.A., Canada, and South Africa, as well as in numerous European countries. Most of these countries were

31   Scottish Blackface Sheep by Loch Lomond.

32   A Rotavator tackles a formidable reclamation job.

33 Massey-Fergusson Tractor with loader filling manure spreader.

34 A Massey-Fergusson three-furrow mould-board plough.

colonized in the second half of the nineteenth century and the first quarter of the twentieth, the earliest recorded shipment to New Zealand occurring in 1853. The breed association was formed in 1895.

THE SOUTHDOWN

The type known as the Southdown in the eighteenth century bore only a slight resemblance to the modern, stocky, small, short-legged animal. Thomas Davis, a Wiltshire farmer who encountered it at the end of the century, describes it as 'a short-legged low sheep, without horns, and generally with black faces and legs; low and light in their fore quarters, but very good in their back and hind quarters; small and light in their heads and necks and offals in general; full of wool, and that wool commonly very fine'. Dr Allan Fraser in his book *Sheep Husbandry* states that the narrow faces were speckled black and white, like a modern Kerry Hill, and that contemporary pictures show a slender, long-legged sheep.

The improver of the Southdown was a farmer, John Ellman, of Glynde, near Lewes in Sussex, who lived from 1753 to 1832. He began his experiments which laid the foundation of the modern Southdown in 1778, and from this beginning was evolved a breed which not only provided much of the basic stock for Australia, U.S.A., Canada, Argentina, Peru and New Zealand, but was also freely used in the development of the other down breeds.

THE HAMPSHIRE DOWN

In 1839 Jonas Webb, of Babraham, in Cambridgeshire, and, next to Ellman, the great improver of the Southdown, exhibited some of his best stock at the first Royal Show. One of the rams was purchased by a Mr Humfrey, of Oak Ash, near Newbury, who used it, by judicious crosses on the old Wiltshire Horn and Berkshire Knot breeds, to produce the first Hampshire Downs. This breed subsequently became immensely popular, as it still is, and has been exported to almost every country in the world.

THE WILTSHIRE HORN

We must refer to the Wiltshire Horn at this point, even though it is now hardly known in the county from which it takes its name. Its story provides a fascinating comment on one of the less successful efforts of the improvers.

In 1811, when Thomas Davis prepared a survey of Wiltshire for the Board of Agriculture, he estimated 500,000 sheep in south Wiltshire alone. W. H. Hudson recorded that in 1840 'a solitary flock of the pure-bred old Wiltshire sheep existed'. Within thirty years it had almost completely disappeared. What happened?

As the process was already beginning when Thomas Davis wrote, that observant old agriculturist can tell us. The primitive Wiltshire Horn was evidently an ungainly animal. It was rather small, lean and scraggy and produced little wool. Both males and females carried a heavy head of horns.

By the time the improvers had finished with it the Wiltshire Horn was a much handsomer animal. It was larger, better proportioned, had been given a fine Roman nose, and its fleece was uniformly white. Unfortunately it had lost the stamina which enabled it to thrive on the bleak downs! And so it had to go.

There is a sequel to the story. Rams of the old Wiltshire Horn breed had been in demand for crossing with the mountain sheep of North Wales for producing early lambs (as their successors still are). This trade was satisfied by certain dealer-farmers of Northamptonshire and Buckinghamshire whose farms were stations on the old drovers' roads. When the Wiltshire supply looked like drying up several of these dealers, and notably one whom Thomas Davis calls 'the much-reputed Mr Westcar', took the precaution of starting ram-breeding flocks of their own. And some of their customers in North Wales did the same.

So if nowadays we examine the exhibits of Wiltshire Horn sheep at agricultural shows we shall find that nearly all of them come from either Northamptonshire and Buckinghamshire or North Wales! In recent years they have developed an export trade, among other places to that other Salisbury in Southern Rhodesia.

THE DORSET HORN

Both the Wiltshire Horn and the Dorset Horn are probably derived from a horned type once widely distributed in the West Country and Wales. The Welsh mountain sheep may be other descendants, as are the primitive Portland sheep, of which a few specimens still survive, I believe, on the Isle of Portland. Richard Carew, who wrote of this ancient type of sheep in Cornwall in 1811, described them as having coarse fleeces but carrying a reasonable amount of flesh and being quite prolific. They put on weight quickly and produced an unusual proportion of twins.

One of the great assets of the modern Dorset Horn, which is serving it well in its present expansion, is its ability, under correct management, to produce three crops of lambs in two years. This same propensity was noted by one Edward Lisle, who travelled in Dorset in the year 1707.

The advent of the Dorset Down caused some decline in the Dorset Horn population in the second half of the nineteenth century, but the breed is now on the upgrade again. A polled strain is being established.

THE DORSET DOWN

The Dorset Down is stated to be the result of crossing Hampshire Down ewes with a Southdown ram in the 1840s. Subsequently it was strengthened by the introduction of certain local characteristics from the native south-western horned sheep, and the Southdown ram may well have had some of this blood in him in the first place. Further crosses may also have been made, but the early history is obscure. The breed is well established and has exported animals to the great sheep-producing countries of the world.

THE DEVON BREEDS

There are five of these, in addition to recent introductions such as the Scottish Blackfaces on Dartmoor. They are the Devon Longwool, Dartmoor, South Devon, Devon Closewool, and Exmoor Horn.

Devon was thickly populated with sheep at the time of the Domesday Book, though nothing is known of their appearance. No doubt the Exmoor Horn, though now improved, represents an aboriginal type.

At some unknown period certain unrecorded introductions had been made to produce a distinct local breed known in the late eighteenth century as the Devonshire Nott, a long-woolled sheep. The new Leicester sheep (see below) were brought in to effect a further improvement, creating in the early nineteenth century a breed called the Bampton. From this were evolved both the Devon Longwool and the Dartmoor; also, probably, the South Devon.

About the same time the Exmoor Horn was also improved. The Devon Closewool is a breed of recent development, originating from the stabilization of a cross between the Devon Longwool and Exmoor Horn. In recent years it has increased in numbers in its native district – the region between Exmoor and Dartmoor – and is now beginning to move into other parts of England.

THE MENDIP

Although no breed of this name is now known, the Mendip Hills of Somerset were from very early times densely inhabited by sheep which were probably a local version of the widely distributed old south-western type and thus resembled the Dorset and Wiltshire Horns. Mendip was in mediaeval times a centre of the wool trade.

THE COTSWOLD

This breed, once virtually supreme in the Midlands, is now almost though not quite extinct. It may well have originated from sheep kept on the numerous large Roman estates in the vicinity of Cirencester. A large, long-woolled breed, the Cotswolds were in the Middle Ages the foundation of the English wool trade. What they looked like we do not know, for in the seventeenth century (and perhaps earlier) breeders began crossing them with Leicesters and other types. With an animal which begins breeding at from one to two years characteristics can be changed very quickly, and the Cotswolds which survived into the nineteenth century (and in small numbers to the present time) may be very different from their ancestors. In general, however, we may say that the Cotswold in its later days was a very large animal, capable of living on rough food and converting it into flesh rapidly. Its meat, however, was coarse and commanded low prices, while the wool quality was surpassed by that of the improved Midland and down breeds. Nevertheless the reason why the Cotswold should be so completely superseded is obscure. It has left its mark on a couple of flourishing meat-producing breeds in North Germany and Holland, and several pure-bred flocks survive in Canada.

THE OXFORD DOWN

This, the largest British breed, is also directly descended from the Cotswold. It was created by Oxfordshire flock-masters in the years from 1830 onwards by crossing improved Hampshire Downs with the Cotswolds. A very versatile sheep, it has found its way to most countries in the world.

The Berkshire Knot

An extinct breed or type which was one of the chief
ancestors of the Hampshire Down, the Berkshire Knot (it was
both polled and horned, in spite of its name) seems to have
resembled the Wiltshire Horn in general appearance. It was
black-faced and made slow growth.

The Leicester

We now come to the key to the whole revolution in sheep-
breeding which transformed the English flocks in the eighteenth
century, the Leicester. This was the breed on which Robert
Bakewell, whom we have already seen in action when considering the great cattle-breeders, started work about the year 1755.

Bakewell used on his sheep the same principles that he
employed with his cattle, but with greater success. His
methods included in-breeding, and he may be honoured as the
pioneer of progeny testing, for he made a practice of letting
out his best rams to his neighbours and selecting the types he
wanted from their progeny.

The old, unimproved Leicester was a long-woolled (or
perhaps by our standards a middle-woolled) type resembling
both the Cotswold and the Lincoln and quite possibly deriving
like them from Roman ancestry. It was widely distributed in
the Midland counties, from Nottinghamshire to Buckinghamshire. Before Bakewell's time a Joseph Allom, of Clifton,
Leicestershire, had done something to improve the breed. No
one knows the sources of the sheep which Bakewell used, but
it is likely that this widely travelled man drew them from
many parts of the Midlands, and it has even been suggested
that at one stage he imported stock from the Netherlands.

The sheep which Bakewell aimed at and succeeded in producing was primarily an early-maturing animal for the
butcher. It proved to be an ideal crossing sheep and left its
mark on almost every breed in the country (and overseas as

well, for the new Leicester became internationally famous).
Indeed, it eventually proved of greater advantage to other
breeds than to itself, for Bakewell's preoccupation with
establishing meat-producing abilities allowed certain other
important characteristics to be lost. The new Leicester tended
to grow overfat, its flesh was not of good quality, it became
less prolific in breeding, and its fleece deteriorated. In the
end it lost favour in its native counties and now survives
chiefly on the wolds of East Yorkshire, although it is represented in many countries overseas.

THE RYELAND

The other formerly great Midland breed of sheep, the
Ryeland, is descended from a type once common along the
Welsh Marcher counties and eastwards into Worcestershire
and Staffordshire. A light, short-woolled, polled sheep has
apparently inhabited this region since Roman times at least
and was responsible for the fleece on which a thriving
mediaeval cloth industry was based. 'Lemster Ore', the wool
from the sheep which grazed around Leominster in Hereford-
shire, was reckoned to be the finest wool in the kingdom.

The Ryeland of the eighteenth century also had a small,
sweet-fleshed carcass which was speedily ruined when the
improvers got to work on it, crossing it with down breeds
to improve its size. Taken from its bleak, austere hills and set
to feed in the vales side by side with larger, coarser breeds
with which it was crossed, it soon became almost indistin-
guishable from them. In consequence it was dismissed by
many farmers as being of little value and came near to
extinction. Fortunately it survived and now fills a useful
niche in the economy of the poorer soils of its native counties.

THE MORFE

This extinct breed was probably nearly related to the
Ryeland, differing from it chiefly in being horned. Its homeland

was the hilly country around Bridgnorth, in Shropshire, where it produced wool little inferior to that of the Ryeland. It is thought to have provided some of the foundation stock for the Shropshire breed.

THE CLUN FOREST

All the outlying hill systems of the Welsh borders, such as the Longmynd, the Long Mountain and Eppynt, had their traditional types of sheep. Most have disappeared or been absorbed, but a few have laid the foundations of breeds which still bear the original name. One is the Clun Forest, originating as a white-faced breed on the Clun Hills, near the border of Shropshire and Montgomeryshire. Unravelling the skein of tangled cross-breeding which led to the development of the modern Clun would be a task to defeat the most patient researcher. Downland breeds probably account for at least half its ancestry, with Shropshire and Southdown perhaps predominating. The result, however, has been encouraging, for the Clun is now well established in much of Midland and southern England and is still extending its territory.

THE KERRY HILL

This is another breed from the same area, originating on the Kerry Hills of Montgomeryshire. The chief ingredients of its ancestry are unknown, but are doubtless well mixed. It may owe more to the Eppynt sheep, which had a black-and-white face like the modern Kerry Hill, than to the aboriginal sheep of the hills from which it takes its name, and Bakewell's Leicesters also played their part. The breed has existed in its present form for about a hundred years and has since the Second World War become established in a number of southern counties.

THE RADNOR

The Radnor, little known outside its native county, has a mixed ancestry very similar to that of the Clun.

THE SHROPSHIRE

Unlike the previous three, which are classified as hill breeds, the Shropshire is officially a down breed. It may well have been founded on the Cannock sheep, of neighbouring Staffordshire, which is said to have been an excellent type resembling the Southdown. It probably owes much, too, to the other local types already mentioned. Leicesters and Southdowns were extensively used in its improvement, which culminated in the 1850s and 1860s in its becoming the most popular breed in England. Although its popularity has since declined, it still holds an important place in the local farming economy and has made its contribution to the flocks of many countries.

Before turning to the mountain breeds of the north and Wales we have a few breeds from the eastern counties to consider.

THE NORFOLK HORN

Norfolk had a very ancient breed of sheep resembling the Wiltshire Horn. It was lean, athletic, black-faced and had a very meagre fleece. The eighteenth-century improvers used all their most derogatory epithets on this ill-favoured sheep, which, however, had several valuable assets. It could live on the poor heaths of Breckland; it was unusually fecund; and its flesh was very sweet. The Norfolk Horn became one of the main ancestors of the Suffolk, to which it bequeathed its black face, and then virtually disappeared from the scene, only one pure flock at present surviving. Unfortunately it also passed on to the Suffolk a susceptibility to the disease scrapie.

THE SUFFOLK

This popular and upstanding down breed was based on a cross made by Arthur Young (see above) in the late 1780s. He used the new improved Southdown rams on Norfolk ewes. After a long period of unpopularity the Suffolk is now probably the downland breed in greatest demand for crossing for fat lamb production, particularly in Scotland.

The Lincoln

The famous Lincoln Longwool, already celebrated and much in demand in other parts of England as early as the thirteenth century, may well have derived from Roman sheep on farms around the city of Lindum. Defoe on one of his tours early in the eighteenth century noted the whole East Midland countryside, from the Humber to Bedford, peopled with immense numbers of these large, heavy-fleeced sheep. The breed was, in fact, very similar to the old unimproved Leicester. It may well have contributed to Bakewell's experiments in producing the new Leicester, which was soon being used in crossing back with the Lincoln.

In the flux of improvement the Lincoln lost some of its size and apparently altered the quality of its wool, but gained on meat quality and early maturity. It eventually settled down, as far as this country is concerned, to be the main breed of its native county, but overseas it had a much more dazzling career. It was discovered that the Lincoln/Merino cross produced wool of an outstanding quality for worsted manufacture, and also, later, a noteworthy carcass for refrigeration. For Australia, New Zealand, South America and a host of other countries this therefore became the ideal dual-purpose breed. Vast numbers were also exported all over the world for experimental crossing with other native breeds. The two most famous breeds deriving from the Lincoln (and in both instances from the Merino as well) are the Australian Corriedale and Polwarth.

The Merino

Although this is not a British breed and is not now found in our islands, it has its place in a history of our agriculture by virtue of experiments made with it here in the late eighteenth and early nineteenth centuries. Much of the wealth of Spain was derived from this superb wool-producing sheep, of which that country is said to have possessed 20,000,000 or more in the sixteenth century.

Merinos probably found their way to England in small numbers quite early in the Middle Ages, but subsequently their export from Spain was prohibited on pain of death. Thereafter a trickle of Merino still came in, by smuggling. In 1789 the King himself (George III) acquired some of this smuggled stock for his farm in Richmond Park.

During the Napoleonic Wars the prohibition was, of course, lifted, and a number of important persons interested themselves in Merino experiments. Imported rams were crossed with a wide range of British breeds, and their female progeny mated back to other Merino rams, this being held to be a foolproof method of establishing a breed of British Merinos. A Merino Society formed in 1811 had Sir Joseph Banks, president of the Royal Society, as its president.

In spite of all the patronage and money lavished upon them, the Merino crosses proved unsatisfactory and eventually died out. They have left their mark, however, in a number of modern breeds.

THE FOREST SHEEP

Until the eighteenth century the forests of the north Midlands possessed allied types of a light-woolled, grey-faced sheep. Among them were the Notts Forest Greyface, the Charnwood Forest, and the Derbyshire Woodland. All have long since died out.

THE LINTON

Coming now to the sheep of the northern hills, we find a primitive type known as the Linton (from the great Scottish market) established from very early times primarily on the

Cumbrian mountains, but extending far and wide over the adjacent high country. Characterized by heavy heads, great spiral horns, shaggy, trailing fleeces and wild behaviour, they are so different from the lowland breeds that some authorities have suggested for them an entirely different ancestry, possibly based on the argali of central Asia. Though now extinct or, rather, merged into various modern breeds, we must mention them here because we shall find ourselves referring to Linton progenitors when we consider the Scottish Blackface, Swaledale and others.

THE DERBYSHIRE GRITSTONE

This breed from the Derbyshire gritstone measures claims to have kept itself pure for over a hundred years. Its origin may lie in the crossing of Scottish Blackface sheep, introduced in the 1840s, with the native Woodland type.

THE TEESWATER

This archaic breed was evolved, perhaps in the seventeenth or early eighteenth century, from the Lincoln, and like its parent was a large, heavy-fleeced and somewhat coarse sheep. Some specimens were huge, there being a record of one weighing over $2\frac{1}{4}$ cwt. They naturally produced a great quantity of wool and were prolific breeders. The Teeswater was one of the breeds taken in hand early by Bakewell's disciples, who effected a refinement and consequent diminution in size which did it no good. It eventually became almost extinct, but has been rescued in recent years from complete oblivion by a few breeders who have sheep descended from the old Teeswater stock.

THE WENSLEYDALE, OR PENISTONE

The Wensleydale is one of the improved breeds developed from the Teeswater, probably crossed with a Blackface. It

became established about 1860 and is very popular in our
northern counties, its cross with the Swaledale or other mountain breed being the well-known 'Masham'.

THE SWALEDALE

Now one of the most numerous sheep in northern England
(being particularly popular as the other half of the 'Masham'),
the Swaledale originated from a mountain sheep of Linton
type inhabiting the watershed between Swaledale and the
vales of Westmorland. It was little touched by early improvers
and remained relatively unknown, except on its native moors,
until the formation of the breed society in 1921.

THE LONK

The Lonk of the central Pennines, particularly of the
Lancashire slopes, is another Linton-based breed, being
descended chiefly from the Scottish Blackface.

THE ROUGH FELL

A relatively unimproved breed ranging the mountains of
Cumberland and Westmorland, the Rough Fell belongs to the
same family as the Scottish Blackface and the old Linton.
Indeed, it is probably nearer the original type than the improved Blackface.

THE HERDWICK

The story that this breed is descended from sheep released
from a wrecked galleon of the Spanish Armada is apocryphal.
Probably it is of Scandinavian origin, the Cumberland Lake
District where it lives owing most of its human population to
immigrant Norsemen. Nowadays it has a rough, shaggy
fleece and is horned, but G. Culley, writing of it from personal
knowledge in 1807, described it as short-woolled and polled.

This original type closely resembled a now extinct breed, the Silverdales, from the Milnthorpe district and must have been greatly altered by crossing with local breeds of Linton derivation.

THE CHEVIOT

The origins of the Scottish breeds are even more confused than those of the English, and an investigation of the old types, flourishing before the eighteenth century, usually leads to speculation. Conflicting accounts are given of the original sheep roaming the Cheviot Hills, some stating that they were horned and some that they were polled, some tan-faced, some black-faced and some white-faced. Late in the eighteenth century a few Cheviot farmers brought in Lincolns and some of Bakewell's new Leicester rams to improve the breed, and the native Cheviot proved to be one of the indigenous types which could absorb this new blood with advantage.

It so happened that the improvement of the Cheviot coincided with the French wars and consequent unlimited demand for wool, in short supply because of the blockade. Most of Scotland being thinly populated by sheep, the Cheviots advanced like a stubble fire, great flocks being sent to the Highland counties, where many of the landowners were then of the opinion that their future lay in large-scale sheep-farming. Later on, in the nineteenth century, the Scottish Blackface returned to much of this territory, which it still occupies, but the Cheviots retained their hold on the northern-most counties of Sutherland and Caithness. The breed is therefore now split into two types, the South Country and the North Country Cheviots; indeed, they are now reckoned as two separate breeds, the North Country Cheviot sheep-breeders having formed a society of their own in 1946.

The modern Cheviot is an excellent producer of both meat and wool and has done well in most sheep-breeding countries of the world.

THE BORDER LEICESTER

Matthew and George Culley were a couple of pupils of Bakewell who introduced in 1767 some of his improved Leicesters to their farm at Fenton in Northumberland. There they established a reputation, maintained by the Culleys' practice of returning again and again to Bakewell's stock to replenish their flock. It is likely, however, that some local blood, probably Cheviot, was also incorporated. From about 1830 onwards the practice of sending south for rams seems to have been discontinued, and thereafter the Border Leicester developed along its own lines, finishing as a very different sheep from the Leicester.

Above all else the Border Leicester is bred for its rams, which are of supreme importance in Scottish sheep-breeding. The Border Leicester ram on the Cheviot gives the celebrated Scottish Half-bred, while the Border Leicester ram on the Blackface gives the equally valuable Greyface.

THE SCOTTISH BLACKFACE

As we have seen, the Scottish Blackface is the direct descendant of the old Linton type of the Pennines, no doubt representing developments from the northern flocks. Like the Cheviot, the improved Blackface had its opportunity in the late eighteenth century, when the Highlands, pacified at last, were beginning to be opened up for farming. For several decades the Cheviot and Blackface contended for the new territory, a struggle in which the Blackface came off best, except, as we have seen, on the southern hills and in the far north. The reason for this distribution was that the Blackface proved able to thrive on heather, whereas the Cheviot needed grass. There are now three types of Scottish Blackface, the Newton Stewart, the Lanark, and the Lewis, but one needs to be an expert to distinguish between them.

THE SCOTTISH WHITE-FACE

There are numerous references to a small, white-faced sheep which inhabited, in small numbers, many parts of the Highlands before the Blackfaces and Cheviots moved in. Most have long since disappeared, though possibly a few survive in remote corners of the Highlands.

THE SHETLAND

Inhabiting the northernmost islands of Britain, the Shetland has the distinction of producing one of our finest wools, widely known as the material from which Shetland knitting and weaving wool is prepared. It is one of our smallest breeds and probably derives from Scandinavian ancestors. Since the formation of its flock book in 1926 it has been much improved and has provided sheep for crossing in kinder climates, but away from the gaunt Shetland moors the quality of the wool quickly deteriorates.

THE SOAY

This very primitive type is thought to be a direct descendant of the sheep kept by Neolithic man. A fleet-footed, dark-fleeced animal, it sheds its wool and was formerly plucked rather than shorn. After surviving on the island of Soay, in the St Kilda group, it has recently been introduced to Ailsa Craig and the Welsh island of Skokholm.

THE LOGHTAN AND OTHER HORNED BREEDS

Four-horned and even six-horned sheep were to be found here and there in the Highlands until at least the early part of the nineteenth century. The only survivors of which I know are the handful of Loghtan sheep on the Isle of Man.

THE WELSH MOUNTAIN

Returning to Wales, we find it inhabited from early times by a race of sheep nearly related to the Wiltshire Horn, Norfolk Horn and other ancient English types. Through the centuries local strains established themselves and, by considerable in-breeding, eventually merited the title of breeds. Some of these still survive, examples being the Rhiw of North Wales, the Cardys of Cardiganshire, and the Talybont. As recently as 1962 a local society was formed for a breed of Pembrokeshire and Carmarthenshire, the Llanwenog.

Although neglected by improvers until late in the eighteenth century, the Welsh Mountain sheep traditionally provided immense numbers of animals, driven along the drovers' tracks, for the London market. As interest grew in stock improvement, however, it not only attracted rams of many of the improved breeds to Wales but also resulted in the establishment of considerable flocks of Welsh sheep on English farms. This was, of course, a development of the system whereby the store sheep of Wales were finished on the fatter land of lowland England, but now many of the ovine immigrants were kept on for breeding, in a wide range of experimental crosses. These breeders had an inkling of what they were after, namely, a good Welsh Half-bred for producing early lambs. Their efforts were not unsuccessful, but the Scottish Half-bred in the end proved a better proposition.

The Welsh Mountain still remains supreme on its native hills, is still a useful crossing ewe, and still has its ancient local races. While much of the stock may retain some of the blood introduced by the improvers of the late eighteenth and early nineteenth centuries, the contribution is most marked in the race or breed centred on the Lleyn peninsula of Caernarvonshire. Lleyn sheep, which are now also found in Anglesey, are based on crosses between the Welsh Mountain breed and Bakewell's new Leicesters.

THE BLACK WELSH MOUNTAIN

The soft black wool of this breed was valued highly back in the Middle Ages, when the blacks which occurred in the Welsh flocks were known as Cochddu. About a hundred years ago Welsh breeders began to collect these blacks together into flocks and to establish them as a distinct breed. The Black Welsh Mountain is thus based on very ancient foundations, although its breed society was formed as recently as 1922. Nowadays it is found not only on its native hills but also in English parks, where it is ornamental as well as useful.

THE ROSCOMMON

English breeds of sheep are common in Ireland, but Ireland has one breed of its own of considerable importance. This is the Roscommon Longwool, which is found chiefly in the counties of Roscommon, Galway, and Longford. It owes its origin to the crossing of the new Leicesters on ancient Irish types and was once very numerous, but has been losing ground in recent years through having too coarse a carcass for the modern market. There is probably Roscommon blood in some Welsh flocks.

PIGS

The short-legged, round-bodied Chinese pig, on which our modern breeds are based, was known to and bred by the Romans, though whether in Britain we cannot say. At the end of the Roman era any surviving domesticated stock doubtless escaped and interbred with the proliferating wild swine. Pigs were probably the most abundant farm stock in Saxon England, as is illustrated by the frequent contemporary references to them and to their swineherds and by the numerous place-names containing the element 'swine' or 'swin'. These, however, were undoubtedly the razor-backed animals of the type which swarmed through the streets of London in the reign of Queen Elizabeth, scavenging for a meagre living. Although mediaeval abbey estates fattened some pigs on cereal mixtures, in general vast numbers of swine derived their living from the woods, where pig-pasturing rights were known as pannage. Pigs being what they are the swineherd must have had an almost hopeless task if he tried to prevent their straying. They doubtless interbred with wild boars and could perhaps be considered as animals of the chase rather than domesticated stock. Such conditions seem to have prevailed in parts of the Highlands until the eighteenth or even the nineteenth centuries.

The proper domestication of the pig was doubtless a protracted process. By the sixteenth century Thomas Tusser writes of castrating and ringing pigs and mentions, with disapproval, the practice of tethering them. Most sows were then apparently farrowing indoors, and some care was being taken of them in sickness. In general, however, the pig was still dependent on woodlands. Well-forested regions had a large pig population, but few pigs are recorded in the relatively treeless districts of the Fens and Salisbury Plain.

As the drovers' traffic developed increasing numbers of Welsh pigs were brought to be fattened on the whey of English cheese-making districts.

THE CHINA PIG

Pigs are reputed to have been domesticated in China for nearly 5,000 years, and, as we have seen, Chinese pigs had found their way to the Mediterranean countries in the days of the Roman Empire. From this stock had developed a number of south European breeds, of which the most important were perhaps the Neapolitan and the Portugal. Small numbers of these seem to have been brought to England before the age of wholesale livestock improvement, for John Evelyn had a

Portugal pig on his estate at Wotton, near Dorking, in the seventeenth century. From 1770 onwards considerable numbers of Chinese pigs were imported into England, some direct from China and others via Italy and in the form of Italian crossbreds. These introductions, though quickly absorbed by the native stock, made important contributions to most of the British breeds eventually developed.

THE SIAMESE PIG

This breed also, from south-east Asia, was known in the Roman world and had its share in the evolution of certain European breeds, notably the Neapolitan. It resembled the Chinese pig in appearance and rotundity, but had black hair (the Chinese was white) with a bronze-coloured skin. In the late eighteenth century pigs of this breed were imported in some numbers direct from Indo-China, notably from the Tonquin region, for which reason they were known as 'Tonquin' or 'Tonkey' pigs. They, too, quickly lost their identity but left their mark by interbreeding with English pigs.

EARLY TYPES OF PIG

By the end of the eighteenth century local types of pig were beginning to emerge, often with the assistance of the imported Chinese and Indo-Chinese stock. One of the commonest was the Berkshire, which was found not only in the county from which it derived its name but also in places as far away as Norfolk, Yorkshire, and Devon, as well as in Ireland. It is described as a large, heavy pig, with short legs and drooping ears, and its colour (though there is conflicting evidence) seems to have been red with black spots. Similar very large, lop-eared pigs, though white in colour, were common in Shropshire, Northamptonshire, and Gloucestershire. These pigs grew to enormous weights and were of much better quality than the contemporary Yorkshire. The Lincolnshire pig, also white, had a curly coat, while the white Suffolk was,

probably through much crossing with the Chinese, distinctly
smaller. Both Hampshire and Essex had black-and-white pigs,
doubtless the ancestors of the Wessex and Essex Saddlebacks
respectively. Wales, Cornwall, and Scotland all had primitive
pigs not far removed from wild swine, though the main Welsh
stock was of a white type, resembling the Midland English,
but with less evidence of improvement.

THE BERKSHIRE

The breed to which Bakewell's stock-breeding methods
were first extensively applied was probably the Berkshire. Its
great improver is said to have been a Lord Barrington, by the
time of whose death in 1829 the breed was recognizable as the
Berkshires we now know. Chinese, Neapolitan, and the old
Berkshire blood seem to have been the main ingredients.

From the 1820s onwards the Berkshires enjoyed a thriving
export trade to America, where, in the corn belt of the Middle
West, they became one of the chief factors in evolving the
celebrated Poland China breed. They also later became
popular in Australia, New Zealand, and Canada, and made
important contributions to the pig stock of Germany, Poland,
and Japan. The first herd book was published in 1885.

THE LARGE WHITE

Obscurity surrounds the origins of the Large White. Some
authorities consider it to have been based on the local Yorkshire type, improved by the introduction of Bakewell's
improved stock from Leicestershire. Others, taking note of the
poor quality of the aboriginal Yorkshire, suggest that it owes
most to pigs brought in from Lincolnshire. The breed
achieved prominence in 1851 when a Keighley weaver, Joseph
Tuley, exhibited some outstanding specimens at the Royal
Show. The first herd book appeared in 1881.

Like the Berkshire the Large White, or Yorkshire as it was
more commonly known in Europe, achieved an important

export trade. Whereas the Berkshires went chiefly to America the Yorkshires were exported to Europe to improve the native breeds. They form a major element in the breeding of most of the pigs in France, Germany, the Baltic countries and especially Denmark.

THE MIDDLE WHITE

This breed is an offshoot of the Large White and the now extinct Small White, probably originating from experiments by Joseph Tuley. It is a pork pig.

THE LARGE BLACK

Large Blacks seem to have been improved to the status of a breed first of all in East Anglia, from black pigs living there. Black pigs were, however, found in other parts of the Midlands and south. Bakewell's improved Leicester pigs were black, and a hundred years later, in the late nineteenth century, a few Dorset breeders evolved a breed, which they called the Black Dorset, from local types. With such a prolific animal as the pig it is comparatively easy to breed new types quickly, and to lose them. Large Blacks have been exported chiefly to Germany and central Europe.

THE ESSEX SADDLEBACK

Although black-and-white pigs were among the original stock of Essex it was not until the present century that the modern Essex Saddleback breed emerged. Neapolitan, Berkshire, and Large White stock all made contributions to its development.

THE WESSEX SADDLEBACK

A saddle-backed pig is known to have lived in Sussex in the early nineteenth century, while Hampshire also had black-and-white pigs. The Wessex Saddleback probably derives from crosses between the two, though doubtless with the admixture of other blood. An 1820 export of Hampshires of this type to Massachusetts formed the foundation for the modern American Hampshires, which are likewise saddlebacked. Although thus a breed of respectable antiquity (as pig breeds go) the Wessex acquired a breed society only in 1919.

THE TAMWORTH

We have seen that red pigs of the original Berkshire type were widely distributed in England early in the eighteenth century. When Lord Barrington had finished with improving his Berkshires he had developed a mainly black pig, but the red unimproved type remained in other districts. The Tamworth seems to have evolved from some of the survivors in Staffordshire. The story of the breed being assisted by the introduction, around 1800, of a red jungle boar from India may be true but is not necessary to account for the foxy coloration. The Tamworth is one of the lesser British breeds numerically, but its contribution to the stock of U.S.A., Canada, Australia, and New Zealand is important.

THE GLOUCESTER OLD SPOTS

This is an old local type elevated to the status of a breed, with a breed society, in 1913. In 1914 representatives were exported to U.S.A., where they played their part in creating the Spotted Poland breed. The Gloucester Old Spots achieved quite a vogue in the 1920s, but are now one of our minor breeds, though in no danger of extinction.

OTHER BREEDS

The most important of other breeds is the Welsh. Founded on the aboriginal Welsh stock it has no history of any substance until the last twenty years. Since the Second World War, however, it has developed its potentialities (largely through the stimulus provided by the success of the Landrace, which breed it resembles) to a remarkable extent.

In Cornwall the National Long White Lop-eared, though little known outside the county, is the favourite breed. A similar animal is the Cumberland, also more or less confined to its own county, as is the Lincolnshire Curly-coat to Lincolnshire.

THE LANDRACE

Swedish Landrace pigs were imported into Britain in 1949 and 1953. Selected by delegations from the National Pig Breeders' Association they fetched unprecedented prices when sold here by public auction. Because of the exaggerated value thus placed on them many of the progeny which should have been culled were kept for breeding, with detrimental effects to the breed. These faults have, however, now been largely eliminated, and the Landrace is, next to the Large White, the most numerous breed in England.

MODERN BREEDING TRENDS

In recent years breeders have begun once again, as in the eighteenth century, to use existing breeds as the basic material for producing new and better ones. Now, however, they have the assistance of the maturing science of genetics. The evolution of a new breed, the Camborough, announced late in 1963, was a triumph of co-operation between geneticists and farmers, backed, it must be mentioned, by farseeing bankers.

HORSES

For most of its history the horse has been hardly an agricultural animal. It has been bred on farms primarily for use elsewhere. Our earliest ancestors hunted it and ate it. Then they rode it and harnessed it to chariots. Finally it descended, quite late in its history, to pulling humble carts and, last of all, the plough. Now, after a few centuries of this menial labour, it has been superseded by mechanical power and is back again at the riding stage.

We have already briefly traced (on page 15) the early history and prehistory of the horse in Britain. Detailed investigation of horse remains from the Roman period, particularly from the forts of Hadrian's Wall, reveal at least six types, ranging from small Celtic ponies, no larger than Shetlands, to the great, heavy cavalry horses. It has been suggested by recent historians that the revival in Britain of the old Roman prowess under the shadowy King Arthur may have depended on the reintroduction of some of these heavy saddle horses from Europe. Hence King Arthur's knights, those cataphracted sixth-century equivalents of armoured tanks which were more than a match for the light-armed Saxons.

From this mixed stock, much of which must have become feral, the Saxon and mediaeval horse must have evolved, though it may well be that a few stud farms survived more or less intact. In the Domesday Book horses are not particularly numerous, and most of those mentioned are evidently used for riding by the better-class folk, but there are a few references to horses employed for harrowing on the farms.

From the early Middle Ages stallions were imported in considerable numbers from the Continent, for almost exclusively military purposes. It was their function to breed the gigantic heavy horses which had to carry a knight in full armour. After English longbowmen had provided an answer to this mighty weapon of war, the trend gradually changed towards lighter horses, but still the emphasis remained on their military value. Early in the eighteenth century a writer commented that there had been so much foreign blood introduced that the true-bred English horse hardly existed, except perhaps in some of the semi-wild types in the remoter regions.

As far as breeds of farm horses are concerned, Arthur

Young, towards the end of the eighteenth century, knew only two breeds, one being the Suffolk and the other 'the large black old English horse' which was later named the Shire.

THE SHIRE HORSE

The breed is based on a heavy type of horse common in the eighteenth century throughout much of Midland England. The earliest stallion of which there is any record was the Packington Blind Horse, who lived at the village of Packington, near Ashby-de-la-Zouch, between 1755 and 1770 and left a considerable mark on the breed. By 1790 the type had been fixed, no doubt by farmers using the methods of their contemporary and neighbour, Robert Blakewell, who may himself have taken a hand in it. Breeders of the nineteenth century made considerable improvements and refinements. The breed society was formed in 1878, at first under the title of the English Cart Horse Society, the name 'Shire' being adopted in 1884.

THE SUFFOLK

The chestnut horses of Suffolk were certainly in possession early in the eighteenth century. A sixteenth-century writer also refers to them, and modern speculation has identified them as the descendants of the horses of that notorious horse-breeding tribe, the Iceni. The eighteenth-century improvers did good work on what was, before their time, a rather coarse, ungainly, slow-moving animal. Suffolks have been exported to and proved their value in a great number of countries, including America, Canada, New Zealand, Australia, South Africa, Argentina, and Russia.

THE CLYDESDALE

Although, as with most breeds of livestock, the Clydesdale was greatly improved by selective breeding in the eighteenth century, the breeders were in this instance continuing a process which had begun much earlier. For at least a hundred years previously local landowners and farmers had been reinforcing the local stock with imported Flemish stallions. A Scottish writer, D. Ure, in 1794 claimed that some of the best draught horses in Europe were bred in Lanarkshire. During the nineteenth century the horizons of the breed were enlarged to include similar types from the neighbouring counties and from as far afield as Cumberland and Aberdeenshire. In the late nineteenth century a considerable export trade developed, notably across the Atlantic.

THE PERCHERON

This is a very recent addition to the British roll of farm livestock, dating only from the First World War. Soldiers in northern France, attracted by the horses they saw in the fields of Normandy and Picardy, began in 1916 to send a few back to Britain. The British Percheron Horse Society was formed in 1918, and for a time the breed enjoyed great popularity, but, of course, the mechanical revolution was too near for it to work out its potentialities to the full. The breed takes its name from the district of La Perche, in eastern Normandy, where it was bred as a heavy military and coach horse.

PONIES

It is not the purpose of this book to provide an account of the development of the pony breeds. From time immemorial local types of pony have ranged free over unenclosed areas such as the New Forest, Dartmoor, Exmoor, the northern fells and moors, Wales, Scotland and the islands. The programme is to round them up annually, brand, castrate when necessary and extract numbers of the young stock for breaking. A proportion has always been diverted to agricultural use. Nowadays the ponies flourish largely through the insatiable demand for saddle horses, particularly for young riders.

POULTRY AND SMALL GAME

As already noted, domestic hens were probably introduced into the farmyard by the Belgae in the first century B.C., primarily for the purpose of cock-fighting. The Romans seem to have managed them on a commercial basis, and hens and geese were abundant from the Saxon period onwards. By the early Middle Ages capons were being produced for the table, and the gooseherd was a familiar member of every manor. Ducks seem to have been introduced as domestic poultry in the thirteenth century, coming here from the Continent. Pigeons also began to be kept on a large scale, for fattening for table, about this time, as numerous mediaeval dovecotes testify. Peacocks and swans were other birds kept domestically for food in mediaeval times. Guinea-fowl were evidently first introduced early in the fifteenth century.

DEVELOPMENT OF EARLY BREEDS OF POULTRY

By the eighteenth century distinct breeds of domestic fowls were beginning to be recognized. In addition to the game birds, the Dorking seems to have been well established, founded, it is said, on some five-toed stock introduced by the Romans. The Poland (with a crested topknot) and the Hamburg were also recognized, the latter being particularly favoured in the North of England. Both had then been established on the Continent for a century or more.

The origins of some of the commoner breeds of poultry are as follows:

THE BRAHMA

Originating in the Brahmaputra region of India, it was first imported to England in the 1850s.

INDIAN GAME

This is a breed of game fowl bred by crossing the local game types in Cornwall and Devon with new blood from the East Indies and from other parts of Britain. It was established early in the nineteenth century.

THE LEGHORN

The breed was developed in Italy, finding its way to America in the 1850s and to England in the following decades. Black and buff Leghorns were evolved in Britain in the 1880s.

THE ANCONA

Another Italian breed introduced to this country in the second half of the nineteenth century.

THE MINORCA

This breed, and the related Andalusian, are descended from the Spanish Castilian fowl and first came to Britain from Spain about 1830.

PLYMOUTH ROCK

Bred first in U.S.A., this breed came to Britain in the 1870s.

WYANDOTTE

This is another American breed, developed from a cross between the Hamburg and the Brahma.

SUSSEX

An English breed, the Sussex is nearly related to the Dorking, but although thus based on an ancient type it did not achieve official recognition till 1903.

RHODE ISLAND RED

As its name suggests, this breed originated in America, being developed in the late nineteenth century from several East Indian breeds. It arrived in England in 1903.

THE ORPINGTON

It derives its name from Orpington, in Kent, where the breed was developed from Black Minorcas, Black Rocks, and Croad Langshans, being first exhibited in 1886.

CROAD LANGSHAN

Its chief importance now lies in the contribution it has made to other breeds. A Chinese breed, it was introduced to Britain in 1872 by a Major Croad.

BARNEVELDER

The village of Barneveld in Holland gives its name to this breed, which was first brought to this country in 1921.

PRESENT USES OF THE BREEDS

From the above brief survey it will be noted that most breeds are of comparatively recent origin. Most of them have their breed societies or clubs, which keep alive the recognized standards, but already the commercial poultry industry has taken another step forward. Commercial breeding has now been concentrated in the hands of a small number of giant enterprises who use the old breeds as bricks – the basic material from which they built up their own special hybrid strains. Highly trained geneticists are employed, and the blending of the ingredients is a top secret.

THE GOOSE

A country proverb says that geese on a farm indicate that

the wife wears the trousers! Its significance depends on the goose providing the wife's pin-money, it being held that only through her intervention would such a filthy creature, so apt to foul pastures, be permitted to live on the farm! That being so, the proverb cannot be a very ancient one, for until the last few centuries the goose, far from being a perquisite of the farmer's wife, constituted an important part of the farm economy. We may reflect that it provided not only meat but also such important mediaeval commodities as goose fat and quills for pens and arrows. The goose population of England must once have been enormous. Tens of thousands were once walked to the London market from the surrounding counties, great droves coming down from the Fens, where interference with breeding geese was one of the chief objections raised by those who opposed the Fenland drainage schemes.

The goose has changed little in all the centuries of its domestication, and relatively few breeds have been developed. William Ellis writing in 1750 suggested that the best geese are produced by crossing the English and Portuguese strains, which indicates some importation. The Toulouse breed, perfected in the Toulouse district of France, was brought over about a hundred years ago. The white Emden likewise owes its origin to the German town from which it derives its name; and the familiar Emden-Toulouse was bred in Britain from crosses between the two. Just when Chinese geese found their way to this country from China is not known.

THE DUCK

Though now greatly outnumbering geese in the British agricultural scene ducks, as we noticed on page 156, were much later in starting. They seem to have been introduced from Europe in the second half of the thirteenth century, and by the following century were well established.

White seems to have been the predominant colour of domestic ducks in early days, though doubtless they interbred

with wild mallards. The Normandy duck which was introduced in the first half of the eighteenth century was probably
the same or similar to the breed we now call the Rouen. About
the same time writers refer to the Muscovy, which originated
not in Russia but in South America, from which continent it
was brought over by the Spaniards. (It is, by the way,
scientifically a goose, not a duck.)

During the nineteenth century the Aylesbury was developed as a table bird from a large white type of duck fattened
by cottagers in the Vale of Aylesbury. The Pekin was imported from China in 1873. In the middle decades of the nineteenth century traders brought back the ancestors of the
Indian runner ducks from Malaya and India, where they are
said to have been bred for over 2,000 years. From Indian
Runner and wild mallard blood the Khaki Campbell was
developed, by a Mrs A. Campbell, of Uley, Gloucestershire,
in 1901.

The process of the development of private strains of their
own by breeders engaged in mass production is now beginning
with ducks, as with the domestic fowl.

The Turkey

By 1550, or less than sixty years after Christopher Columbus first set foot on American soil, the turkey was common
throughout much of Europe. Who first brought it here from
its American homeland is uncertain. Some give the credit to
the early Spanish explorers who followed Columbus, others to
Cabot in 1497 and 1498. Yet others put the introduction as
late as 1518. Thomas Tusser writing in 1573 refers to turkeys
as evidently quite common. Turkeys were found in their wild
state along the Atlantic seaboard of America, from New
England to Mexico.

By the eighteenth century a turkey-producing industry had
become concentrated in East Anglia (one of its present-day
centres), from which immense numbers were driven, on foot,

to the London market. Two types, or breeds, are mentioned, the Norfolk and the blue Virginian. Whether they bore any close resemblance to modern breeds is uncertain, for the modern Norfolk Black was developed about 1865, at the same time as a breed known as the Cambridge Bronze, from which the Mammoth Bronze and later types were evolved.

Since the Second World War new strains have been created, largely by commercial breeders working on a very large scale, as with fowls and ducks.

The Guinea-fowl

Although reintroduced to Europe presumably by Portuguese explorers probing along the Guinea Coast in the fifteenth century, the Guinea-fowl had been known and domesticated in Mediterranean countries by the Romans and Greeks. Little has been done to alter it, either in performance or appearance, during the past five hundred years.

The Pigeon

Pigeons, while providing a useful source of fresh meat for the lord of the manor's table in mediaeval times, were so abundant as to be a serious nuisance to his tenant farmers. Pigeon lofts also provided a valuable quota of manure. They continued popular until the early nineteenth century, but are now kept purely for ornament. The American system of force-fattening squab pigeons commercially never caught on here.

OTHER DOMESTIC LIVESTOCK

Rabbits

Rabbits seem to have died out in most of Europe, where they were formerly widespread, during the Ice Ages and to have recolonized it from surviving pockets around the

Mediterranean, the earliest of which to have written mention is Corsica. There is no evidence at all of rabbits being introduced to Britain in Roman times (when they were kept under domestic conditions in Italy), and although the Normans are popularly supposed to have brought them here the first references are no earlier than the thirteenth century. For a long time they were kept in specially contrived warrens, and prices indicate that they remained fairly low in numbers till the sixteenth century. Throughout the Middle Ages therefore the rabbit has at least as sound a claim to be a farm animal as the pig. Early in the seventeenth century some were being specially fattened in large hutches.

Warrens remained a profitable investment till at least the eighteenth century, George Culley recording in 1786 one in the Vale of Pickering, Yorkshire, which was let for £300 a year. From the beginning of the years of depression in the 1870s down to the advent of myxomatosis in 1953 rabbits had proliferated to such an extent in the wild that there was no incentive to large-scale commercial production, though each successive war saw an increase in interest in backyard rabbit-keeping. It was during this period that the domestic breeds, such as the Beverens, Flemish Giant, Belgian Hare, Chinchilla, Havana, and Angora, became familiar.

During the past decade efforts have been made, with some success, to establish a mass-production rabbit industry on the lines of modern poultry enterprises. Special new strains of rabbits, mostly based on the New Zealand white, are being evolved.

THE GOAT

From Neolithic times, when they may have outnumbered sheep, goats have gradually declined in economic importance in this country. Though still plentiful in the Roman era, they seem to have been little favoured by the Saxons, who preferred sheep, and they lingered longest in the Celtic west.

They were kept both for milk (to be drunk neat or made into cheese) and meat, with hair as a by-product for rope manufacture and the making of a coarse hair cloth. Considerable droves of goats were to be found here and there as late as the seventeenth century, but there are few references to them a hundred years later.

Reviving interest in the second half of the nineteenth century led to the formation of the British Goat Society in 1879. New types of goats were introduced, resulting in the establishment of such breeds as the Anglo-Nubian, Saanen, and British Alpine. These make a brave display at agricultural shows and give impressive yields of milk, but their function is mainly that of producing milk for their owners' households.

THE ASS

Donkeys were used by the Romans for agricultural work but thereafter seem never to have been of any great importance. In Saxon and Norman times they appear to have been rare. The eighteenth century saw them in use, here and there, for light cultivations and traction work and, in Devon, as pack animals. They were often milked, and I have talked with people who remember seeing asses being milked in the streets of London, asses' milk being presumed to have valuable medicinal qualities.

THE DOG

This animal we will consider only in its agricultural aspect, which eliminates sporting dogs, fancy dogs and most modern breeds developed mainly as pets.

From very early times dogs were valued for their work both in managing sheep and cattle and in protecting them from wild animals. The Venedotian Code of ancient Wales mentions three types of dog, the shepherd dog, the mastiff and the house cur. The mediaeval shepherd, to judge by Glastonbury records, was allowed a plot of land for maintenance for his dog. Mediaeval and early sheep-dogs and house-dogs were naturally very large and fierce, but with the disappearance of wolves they tended to be bred for speed and intelligence rather than weight. Seventeenth-century writers testify to the control exercised over sheep-dogs by means of whistles and other signals from the shepherd.

By the eighteenth century the two main types of sheep-dog seem to have been well established. These were the collie in the North and big, shaggy, bob-tailed dogs of the Old English Sheep-dog pattern in the South. Terriers were well known as sporting dogs, and so were greyhounds. Most others seem to have been crosses, either deliberate or careless, between these basic types.

The Cat

Cats were probably introduced to Britain by the Romans and later became particularly popular among the Celts. Ancient Welsh codes contain frequent references to cats, of which a quota was required by law to be kept in every group of houses, and severe penalties were enacted for killing them. In Saxon and early mediaeval times cats do not appear to have been plentiful, and weasels were sometimes kept instead, as mousers. Gradually, however, the references increase, and Tusser regarded a cat as an essential item of farm equipment. The cat's real testing-time came with the arrival of the brown rat, which first appeared in Britain about 1730. The battle between these two species is still in progress.

Bees

Although bees may seem to have no place in a treatise on modern agriculture, they do in a survey of agricultural history. Until supplies of sugar became available from overseas, honey was the only source of sweetness on the menu, and bees consequently were one of the most important departments of the farm from time without mind. The folk-lore of all the northern nations is full of references to bees, honey and especially to mead and the other drinks which can be made from honey, and some of the earliest classical writers on agriculture, such as Virgil, devote long sections to bee-keeping.

After being practised as a well-developed art in Roman times, bee-keeping probably fell into neglect and had to be learnt all over again by the Saxons. By the time of the Domesday Book bees on many manors are cared for by specialist bee-keepers, and rents are paid in honey. Bee-keeping flourished throughout the Middle Ages, though its economic importance later declined with the availability of sugar. In the middle years of the nineteenth century the writings of Darwin drew the attention of farmers to the importance of bees in fertilizing crops. Later in the century modern methods of bee-keeping, and in particular the modern beehive, began to be developed, and progress was aided by the formation of the British Bee-keepers' Association in 1874.

Though no longer reckoned as part of the general farm, bees are still highly valued by specialists in clover-production and by fruit-growers, who habitually pay bee-keepers to place colonies of hives in the orchards at blossom-time. Recently Russian scientists have suggested that bees deposit on clovers and grasses a protein which plays an important part in the digestibility of the herbage.

New Food for Farm Animals

Although we have now surveyed fairly comprehensively both our farm animals and the foods traditionally grown for their food, we have yet to consider supplementary foods which have become available for them within the past two hundred years or so.

The great stock-breeding revolution which has occupied our attention throughout this chapter coincided with the intro-duction of oilcake. As a by-product from the extraction of linseed and rape-seed oil, it was first considered as a manure, and Coke of Holkham himself continued to use it as such until towards the end of the eighteenth century. In the 1760s, however, farmers began to appreciate its value as a cattle food, first because it enriched the manure left behind by the animals and then for its effect on the performance of the fattening beast. Soon progressive farmers everywhere were using it, and experiments were going on to discover the possibilities of other 'concentrates'. Some mixed whole linseed, soaked in warm water, with chaff; others chopped up oats and oat-straw together to form a nutritious kind of chaff. The nutritional value of brewers' grains, where available, now began to be appreciated.

Early in the nineteenth century scientists set about analysing the nutritional requirements of animals and the chemical composition of food. Much of the original research was undertaken in Germany, where A. D. Thaer, in a work published in 1809, calculated the nutritional value of a number of feeding-stuffs in comparison to hay. Carbohydrates, proteins and other components were described, and by 1860 German scientists were able to lay down precise theoretical formulae for fattening an ox. Before the end of the century the two functions of food, namely, maintenance and production, were elucidated. The German, O. Kellner, in 1905 published his standards of starch equivalents and protein equivalents, on which almost all subsequent nutritional work has been based.

Meantime farmers were pressing on with their own experiments, often towards culs-de-sac. A cult of fermentation of foodstuffs arose in the middle of the nineteenth century, based on the growing practice of steaming a mixture of chaff, chopped roots and hay and then stirring it up with a concoction of boiled oilcake. It had some value in breaking down the fibrous part of the ration.

What these farmers were, in fact, doing was compounding. They were taking sundry ingredients and trying to weld them into a satisfactory ration. In the latter half of the nineteenth century millers began to do this for them. Joseph Thorley, of

King's Cross, London, was one of the first in the field; he was producing his compound cattle food at Hull in 1856. Another pioneer was the Kingston Cattle Food Company, which was established, also at Hull, in 1853. Its early advertisements have a modern ring with their references to the 'highly condensed compound of pure, nutritious and fattening meals [for cattle] combined with valuable tonic, aromatic, stomachic, and gently stimulating agents'.

In 1869 James Cunningham of Leith was including cottoncake, ground locust and bruised maize in his cattle foods, and in the early 1870s the first shipments of decorticated cottoncake arrived in Britain. By the turn of the century the analysis of the compounds was becoming complex, a fattening meal prepared in 1907–8 by the Phoenix Mill, Liverpool, containing sixteen separate ingredients. By this time, however, it was realized that what mattered was the protein and starch equivalent content – the actual components which contained the nutritional elements being of minor importance.

Since then new ingredients have been added, such as hormones, antibiotics, vitamins and trace elements, some of which have been found necessary to the health of stock under all conditions, but some of which simply enable the animal to survive (until its early slaughter date) under the highly unnatural environments to which it is now subjected.

7

THE STORY OF OUR
FARM IMPLEMENTS

*Tools of cultivation – Tools for sowing and planting –
Tools for harvesting – Tools for the processing of crops
– Tools for land reclamation and maintenance – Tools
for use with livestock – Transport – Power*

THIS increasingly complex subject has developed from a few
simple basic tools. They may be classified as follows:

1. Tools of cultivation.
2. Tools for sowing and planting.
3. Tools for harvesting.
4. Tools for the processing of crops.
5. Tools for land reclamation and maintenance.
6. Tools for use with livestock.
7. Transport.
8. Power.

TOOLS OF CULTIVATION

The simplest implement for cultivating the soil is, of course,
the branch of a tree dragged over the surface, perhaps of land
cleared by fire. Other tools in use from the earliest age of
cultivation must have been the antler and the mattock – the
latter for breaking clods. The plough may have evolved from
a type of hoe which was pushed rather than pulled, a matter on
which we have already speculated on page 17.

PLOUGHS

The Celtic plough of pre-Roman days had no mould-board

and therefore dug a straight furrow without turning over the soil. This accounts for the roughly square shape of the small Celtic fields so numerous in archaeological maps based on air photographs and still discernible from the ground in many downland areas. With such a plough it was necessary to plough the ground a second time, at right-angles to the first furrow. It was therefore an advantage to have all sides of the field equal in length.

Furrow-turning ploughs were introduced by the Belgae in the first century B.C., though they had been known on the Continent at least three hundred years earlier. These heavy ploughs, drawn by several pairs of oxen, had a mould-board, a coulter in front of the plough-share, and a wheel. They thus differed little from a type in use until very recent times (and still to be seen in a few places).

One effect of using them was to alter the shape of the fields from a square to an elongated rectangle, there being not only no need for cross-ploughing but also every inducement to let the lumbering team plod on for as far as possible before turning. Another result was to open up many lowland areas of stiff though fertile soils which had been beyond the capacity of the light Celtic plough.

Both types of plough were used in Roman times. The Romans themselves were used to a light, two-ox plough known as the *aratrum*, but on the larger estate the heavy *caruca* was still employed. The standard Roman land unit, the *jugerum* (roughly two-thirds of an acre) measured 120 feet by 240 feet; and 120 feet was the length of the Roman furrow as ploughed by the *aratrum*.

As the Belgae were in possession for such a short time before the Roman invasion, and then only of the south-eastern section of England, we may conclude that over much of the country the light Celtic plough continued to be employed or, at most, was superseded by the somewhat similar *aratrum* during the Roman centuries. This accounts for the outlines of so many of the Celtic fields being left intact. When Saxon England begins to emerge from the mists of the Dark Ages we find the same two types of plough in use. Although the Saxons are often given credit for introducing the great eight-ox plough, not only were they continuing a practice which had been followed for at least five hundred years but we can see in early Saxon manuscripts the ploughman using a lighter sort of plough as well. History is seldom simple.

Throughout the Middle Ages we see illustrations of men using both light and heavy ploughs, ploughs with or without wheels, with or without coulters and of sundry shapes and patterns. Indeed, when agricultural writers began to study more closely the implements of cultivation in the eighteenth century one of their criticisms was that there were too many types of plough. Each region, each district, seemed to have evolved its own type.

Most of the ploughs then were made largely of wood, reinforced by iron, though with iron plough-shares. The importance of the plough-share is illustrated by the fact that Edward Lisle, writing at the very beginning of the eighteenth century, found that most of the shares in Leicestershire were made from imported Danish iron, English iron being considered less durable and more brittle. Metal shares had, incidentally, been known for many centuries; what appear to be bronze plough-shares from the Bronze Age have been discovered.

The early eighteenth-century writers, too, noted as a novelty ploughs with iron mould-boards, and Arthur Young found in Essex (and introduced to the Society of Arts) the first plough made entirely of iron. Until the middle of the eighteenth century ploughs were locally made by blacksmiths, but thereafter they gradually became factory products, one of the first factories being at Rotherham, where a type known as the Rotherham plough was made. Robert Ransome, founder of the firm which still bears his name, took out a patent for tempering cast-iron shares in 1785.

Both double-furrow and swing-head ploughs were known,

to judge from illustrations in Walter Blith's book, *English Improvers Improved*, as far back as about 1650. A good deal of work was done on improving them during the second half of the eighteenth and first half of the nineteenth centuries, the scientific approach being strongly encouraged during the latter years of the period by the Royal Agricultural Society of England. Gradually, as the Victorian era progressed, the demand for wooden ploughs dwindled (though they were still in use, to my knowledge, in the 1930s). Different types of iron plough for special work, such as digger ploughs and skimming ploughs, were developed, and the number of plough patents in the later years of the nineteenth century is very large. Nevertheless there was, and has been, little basic change in the design of the plough, which is essentially a simple tool. As we shall notice later (see page 193), the era of experiment with steam tackle saw a temporary interest in ploughs with multiple furrows, an interest which has been revived with the introduction of modern powerful tractors. For general work, however, the advantage still seems to be with ploughs of two, three or four furrows drawn at a fair pace rather than with multiple-furrowed juggernauts pulled at a snail's rate by excessively heavy crawler-tractors.

One of the most important features of recent years has, of course, been the hydraulically operated mounted plough, so much more manoeuvrable than the trailer type.

HARROWS AND CULTIVATORS

Harrowing serves three primary purposes: to break up soil into a fine tilth, to bury seed, and to destroy weeds. A thorn bush makes a harrow of sorts and was evidently, from old Celtic references, still used in historic times, though light harrows were also known from a very early date. The Roman *tribulum* (from which is, graphically, derived our word 'tribulation'), though apparently designed for use as a threshing implement, could almost be termed a prototype harrow and may have been used as such. It was a heavy sledge studded on the underside with stumpy projections of iron (or sometimes wood or flint) drawn over a threshing-floor to knock the grain from the ears, and one can easily visualize how it could be adapted to land work.

The Bayeux Tapestry and other mediaeval works of art depict peasants at work with harrows that are very substantially made, consisting of a heavy frame of timbers studded with formidable spikes. They are drawn by sturdy horses. Almost identical implements can be found on some farms today.

The chief improvements made in this simple implement have been in the shape of the frame. From being a massive square it has been developed in triangular, rectangular and rhomboidal models, many of them lighter than the old types. As with ploughs, one of the most important and very recent developments has been that of a hydraulically operated mounted harrow.

Curved-tine harrows (such as the spring-tined model) and cultivators probably derive from the horse-rake, or they may have been developed partly from Jethro Tull's horse-hoe. Cultivators of sorts were being used early in the nineteenth century, since when there have been no radical changes in their pattern.

ROLLERS

Mattocks, for pulverizing clods, must have been one of the earliest agricultural implements. When they began to be replaced by rollers is not known, but mediaeval writers mention stone rollers, specimens of which may still be seen on farms, particularly in the West Country. These stone rollers are cylinders of stone revolving around a spindle set in a hole bored longitudinally. Similar wooden rollers were made from tree-trunks. The Rev. Philip Wright, whose book *Old Farm Implements* was published in 1961, recalls seeing such a wooden roller and records that sometimes they were spiked with iron or encircled with iron rings. The first cast-iron roller appeared about 1800. Until this time mattocks, or beetles, were still being used extensively, many of them being made of or bound with iron, but with the appearance of manu- factured rollers the hand implements gradually disappeared. The earliest ring-rollers seem to have had alternate cylinders of wood and iron, and several very heavy rollers, called clod- crushers, were evolved in the early days. Philip Wright also mentions a 'levelling-box', which resembles a small iron sledge with handles, which apparently was dragged over the fields for the same purpose as a roller.

ROTARY IMPLEMENTS

The middle decades of the nineteenth century saw a lively interest in the development of rotary implements, particularly for use with steam tackle. The earliest device (and incidentally one of the most elaborate) seems to have been one for which a Major Pratt took out a patent in 1810. It appears to have set out to do almost everything in the matter of cultivation, but there is no evidence that it ever got beyond the paper stage. In the 1840s and 1850s numerous patents were filed for rotary diggers, and the subject occupied many pages in the *Journal* of the Royal Agricultural Society. Most of the inventions, however, had the handicap that they were designed for use with a stationary source of power, either horse or steam, anchored at one end of a field, an arrangement which en- countered almost insurmountable difficulties on uneven ground. The principles of rotary tillage could not really be perfected until the coming of the internal-combustion engine.

TOOLS FOR SOWING AND PLANTING

'Behold a sower went forth to sow; and when he sowed, some seeds fell by the wayside, and the fowls came and devoured

them up; some fell upon stony places, where they had not
much earth; and forthwith they sprang up because they had no
deepness of earth; and when the sun was up, they were
scorched; and because they had no root, they withered away.
And some fell among thorns, and the thorns sprang up and
choked them; but others fell into good ground, and brought
forth fruit, some a hundred fold, some sixty fold, some thirty
fold. . . .'

Such were the principles and expectations of the sower from
time immemorial. He sowed the seed by hand, carrying it in a
basket slung across his breast. This method was still in
occasional use in the 1920s and 1930s, though the grain was
more frequently carried in a seed-lip, made either of plywood
or galvanized iron and shaped to fit one's body. I myself have
sown both seed and manure with the aid of this utensil,
though very inexpertly, I fear. A good sower paced the ground
with measured tread, throwing out the grain in unvarying
rhythm, so that an even distribution was achieved. An
elaboration was the seed-fiddle, which, by a simple apparatus
consisting of a bow attached to a revolving disc in a wooden
frame, achieved the same even spread of seed by mechanical
means.

In spite of the sower's skill, the scattering of seed broadcast
is a wasteful method, as the parable quoted declares. 'One for
the pigeon; one for the crow; one to wither; and one to grow',
is the proverbial and probably accurate summary of the ratio
of loss. An obvious way of reducing waste is by the placement
of seed, an idea which has resulted in the invention and re-
invention of seed-drills, dibblers and similar devices during
the past four or five thousand years. Although in this country
credit is usually given to Jethro Tull (1674–1741) for invent-
ing the seed-drill, a somewhat similar machine was certainly
used by the ancient Babylonians, while the Chinese seed-drill
is stated to date from about 2800 B.C.! Seed-drills of sorts are
said to have been employed by several ancient Mediterranean
civilizations, including the Roman, and in modern times a

35   Massey-Fergusson 711 Potato Harvester.

36   Giant Matador Harvester. Note commanding position of the operator and long reach of the discharge auger.

37 Combine harvesters at Well Bottom, near Chicklade, Wilts.

38 Massey-Fergusson 703 straw baler.

Venetian, Camillo Torello, took out a patent for a seed-drill in 1566.

Tull himself was an Oxford graduate who, through ill health, retired to the country and became immersed in rural life. Among his recreations was the playing of the church organ on Sundays, and his inspiration for a seed-drill was based on the church organ pipes. Although one might have suspected that the invention of the seed-drill led to the development of a horse-hoe, for inter-row cultivations, it actually happened the other way round. Tull, having become an almost fanatical advocate of his beloved horse-hoe, invented the seed-drill as an aid to a system of cereal-growing which would allow his horse-hoe to be used.

We need not doubt Tull's claim that he had not read any scientific agricultural books before he made his invention, but nevertheless a good deal of work had been done along the same lines before his time. Following the inventions of Torello and his successors in Italy, English farmers were experimenting with a wide range of machines throughout the seventeenth century. One of these machines, described by a certain J. Sha, whose book was published in 1646, was actually designed to sow seed and manure side by side in almost exactly the same manner as the modern combine-drill. However, there is nothing to indicate that any machine was ever made to this design, and a rather cumbersome seed-drill designed by John Worlidge a little later in the century failed to work when a prototype was made in 1727. So Jethro Tull's seed-drill may claim to be the first English model which worked efficiently, and it was, indeed, so well designed that the basic principles have been little altered to the present day.

Experimentation and steady progress continued throughout the eighteenth century, and when, in 1839, the English Agricultural Society held its first show at Oxford the implement exhibits included a combined seed-and-manure drill for turnips. The 1840s also saw the introduction of drills for sowing lime and soot, and several, that of Thomas Huckwale in 1842 being perhaps the earliest, for distributing liquid manure with the seed. An endless belt of cups ladled out the liquid manure from a tank and poured it down the seed funnel in this somewhat abortive machine.

HOEING

Between seedtime and harvest the farmer's main task is to help his crop combat competition from weeds. Until crops were sown in drills, the only method of weed control was by hand-pulling or by using such primitive implements as sickles or cutting hoes to cut them. Jethro Tull's horse-hoe was not therefore the development of a horse-drawn implement to replace one which had formerly been used by hand; rather, it was an entirely new conception of husbandry (though Robert Trow-Smith in his *English Husbandry* suggests that Tull may have got the idea from a tour of France, where he saw the French method of inter-row cultivation in vineyards). Oddly enough, it was based on a completely erroneous theory.

Tull reasoned that, of the five elements of which, according to the ancients, matter was composed (namely, earth, air, water, fire and nitre), only earth provided nourishment for plants. Plants must therefore feed on minute particles of earth. Hence the secret of successful husbandry was to break the earth into as small particles as possible. So he invented the horse-hoe. And, in order to create the right conditions for his horse-hoe to work, he invented the seed-drill. Seldom can such important developments have followed from such a complete misunderstanding.

Tull used to sow his wheat in double-drills, with 5-feet gaps between each pair of drills. He also intercropped his wheat-fields with turnips, which he pulled in spring. He thus prepared the way for his great successor, Viscount Townshend, who in 1730 began that remarkable career on his Norfolk estates which resulted in the establishment of the Norfolk four-course rotation.

TOOLS FOR HARVESTING

Modern farmers do not need to be reminded that cereals are only one of the crops to be harvested, but as harvest for most people means primarily the corn harvest we will deal with that first.

The traditional tools for harvesting are the scythe and the sickle. Although in the years immediately prior to the present age of mechanization the scythe was in far more frequent use, it is likely that the sickle was more specifically designed for corn, the scythe being an all-purpose tool, particularly useful for mowing long grass. The true sickle differs from the modern reap-hook in having a serrated edge. Most ancient civilizations seem to have adopted the practice of removing the ears of the corn first and dealing with the straw later, and the conventional method of using the sickle is to grasp a handful of ears with one hand and sever their stalks by drawing the tooth-edged blade across them.

A mechanical reaper was invented by the Romans. It is described by both Pliny, in the first century A.D., and by Palladius, in A.D. 391, who says:

'A cart is constructed, moved on two wheels – the boards in front being lower than the rest, and on that part a great number of teeth are fitted in a row at intervals. An ox is yoked to two poles and harnessed head towards the cart, so that he pushes it into standing corn. The driver walks with the ox and regulates the height and depth of the teeth frame.'

How extensively this machine was used is not known, and mediaeval and later references to it may simply imply that the author had read his classics and not necessarily that he had any knowledge of the device. Towards the end of the eighteenth century the idea attracted attention, and several attempts were made to reconstruct the machine. Thereafter inventors multiplied, the number of designs tested being equalled by the rapidity with which they failed. There were machines with circular blades, with semicircular blades and with twelve-sided blades; machines in which separate blades, resembling those of sickles or scythes, were mounted on sundry ingenious bases; machines which were pushed and machines which were pulled; machines which spoiled their good efforts by running over the corn as soon as it had been cut; and machines which would work only on level ground.

Credit for the first practical mechanical reaper is usually given to Cyrus McCormick, a Virginian farmer who, following some unsuccessful experiments made between the years 1816 and 1831, produced his machine about 1840. The design was greatly improved by further patents in 1845 and attracted considerable publicity at New York's Great Fair in 1851. However, a prior claim may be made out for Rev. Patrick Bell, of Carmylie, Forfarshire, who produced a reaper which can be regarded as a prototype of the modern machine in 1826. His invention was taken up by the Highland and Agricultural Society, who paid him a premium of £50. By 1832 ten of the machines were working in Scotland, where in that year they harvested 320 acres, while others had been exported to Poland and Tasmania. Bell himself was unduly modest about his invention, which he refused to patent. No manufacturer came forward to take it up, and the idea was neglected till after the success of McCormick's machine.

Like Jethro Tull with his seed-drill, Bell claimed that he had not been influenced by the work of any of his predecessors. All that he had ever seen was a picture of a reaper invented by a Mr Smith, of Deanston, whose machine worked on an entirely different principle, its cutters being blades attached to a disc fixed horizontally on the bottom of a revolving drum. Bell evolved his machine from the action of scissors, a theory which proved to be the correct one.

We thus find, as so often happens in the history of discovery and invention, two men working independently in different countries at approximately the same time. Although their investigations may have been completely independent of previous experiments, as Bell claimed, one usually finds that a crowning achievement of this sort comes as an appropriate climax to a period of effort, involving much trial and error, by a considerable number of workers. It can be said that when the time is ripe a climate of culture is created in which someone or other is almost certain to produce what is required.

From 1851 onwards progress was steady. By 1879, when McCormick won a Gold Medal offered by the Royal Agricultural Society of England, the principles of a string-tying binder had been mastered, chiefly by research in America. In the 1890s the binder-reaper, or self-binder, began to come into general use. In America and Canada the next step was to combine the reaping-machine with the threshing-machine, thus producing the combine-harvester, which first came across the Atlantic to this country about 1926. This machine was not widely used in Britain till the Second World War, and, although it is now almost universally employed, improvements are still being made.

HAYMAKING

Although there is much overlapping in the processes of harvesting corn and harvesting hay, the essential haymaking tools are the scythe, the pitchfork and the rake. As far as the cutting of grass for hay is concerned, the scythe and sickle remained unchallenged until the invention of the reaper in the nineteenth century. This new machine could obviously be used equally efficiently for grass as for corn; indeed, the former crop presented fewer problems.

The second operation of haymaking, namely, the drying of the grass for conservation, is much more complicated, especially in the British climate. It is a matter of turning and tedding the hay, spreading it in the elusive sunshine to dry, and then snatching it into rick or barn before the storms catch it. So long as labour remained cheap and plentiful, these were operations perhaps best done by hand, and therefore mechanical aids were late in coming on the scene. No record exists of the invention of the first horse-rake. Arthur Young mentions seeing one in use in Essex in 1807, where it was being employed in raking up bean straw, but there is nothing to indicate whether this was an innovation or not.

Tedders of sorts, of unknown origin, were being used in Middlesex at the end of the Napoleonic Wars and by the 1830s seem to have been in fairly general use. The Royal Agricultural Society held its first trial of haymaking machines in 1846, when one, made by H. Smith & Company of Stamford, which could be raised and lowered at will, won an award of £5. Later in the century interest switched to the development of swathe-turners, both these and side-rake being perfected in the first decade of the present century.

Hay-loaders, of which old horse-drawn specimens can still be found mouldering in farmyards, attracted a good deal of attention in the last quarter of the nineteenth century. The hay-sweep, from which was evolved the buck-rake, was introduced from America in 1894, as was the baler in 1880, when the first examples were exhibited at the Royal Show at Derby.

Balers were first regarded as an adjunct of the threshing-machine or as barn or farmyard equipment. There are references to them in American literature as early as 1813, and an inventor named H. L. Emery began making them at Albany, New York, in 1853. From 1860 onwards two other manufacturers, P. K. Dederick and George Ertel, were devoting most of their time to the development of hay-balers. Portable balers were in use in America as long ago as 1870, but the first commercial pick-up baler was manufactured there by J. I. Case & Company in 1933. Lend-lease during the Second World War really started the flow to Britain.

As with most machines, the baler had to await the perfection of the modern tractor before it could entirely fulfil its promise. Similarly, the technique of silage-making is said to have been known as long ago as the reign of the first Queen Elizabeth, but was little practised until towards the end of the nineteenth century. It owes its post-war popularity largely to the sudden availability of the tractor-mounted, hydraulically operated buck-rake, and, of course, the even later introduction of the forage-harvester. This last machine is so recent that few British farmers had ever set eyes on one till 1958.

HARVESTING ROOT-CROPS

Farmers who grow turnips, swedes and mangolds still either pull them by hand or allow livestock to eat them where they grow. Sugar-beet and potatoes are the only widely grown root-crops of which the harvesting has attracted the attention of the engineer.

Little interest was taken in the mechanical harvesting of potatoes until the second half of the nineteenth century, and progress in developing potato-harvesters really began with the very large compulsory increase in the potato acreage during the Second World War. Early efforts were directed to producing machines of the spinner type, the revolving tines of which threw the tubers out of the ground. More recently elaborate machines have been designed, and are still being designed, for lifting, sorting and bagging potatoes.

Similar development has occurred with the harvesting of sugar-beet, though, of course, even less time has been available, since sugar-beet did not become thoroughly established as a British crop till the 1920s. This being a valuable crop, it has attracted a good deal of research and ingenuity, directed along two lines. One has been to design a large, all-purpose machine which lifts, tops and cleans the beet and loads them into trailers. The other concentrates on several relatively inexpensive machines, each of which does only one job but does it well. Some fairly efficient machines of both types are now available, though there is still room for improvement.

Both sugar-beet- and potato-harvesters are concentrated largely in the Fens and other regions of intensive cultivation in the eastern counties. Here, where market-garden crops are grown on a field scale, there has also been a development of machines for planting such crops as brassicas, leeks and, of course, potatoes.

TOOLS FOR THE PROCESSING OF CROPS

Under this heading I propose to consider simply such after-harvest treatment of crops as occurs on the farm. Cereal crops must naturally be our first interest.

THRESHING

The inclusion of threshing as a post-harvest operation is, of course, anachronistic, for the whole process is now carried out, on most farms, by the combine-harvester in the field. As we have noted, however, this is a very recent development, and until the present century threshing has always been a separate task, often carried out long after harvest.

The traditional threshing implement is the flail (constructed, incidentally, of two crab-apple staves linked by an eelskin thong). Because of our climate, threshing was carried on, even in prehistoric times, in great barns rather than out of doors. The Romans introduced their own threshing implement, the *tribulum*, which we have already mentioned when dealing with harrows, but this heavy, ox-drawn sledge was really more suitable for work in the open air and probably had a limited application in Britain. Nevertheless, according to the evidence of monastic records it survived in a few places till early mediaeval times. And, although the flail was the most universally used method, here and there threshing was done by treading the corn with oxen, or even with men, on a sheet or threshing-floor.

Much grain was still being threshed by flail at the end of Queen Victoria's reign, but by then threshing-machines had been in existence for more than a hundred years. One of the fruits of the great era of agricultural progress which began in the eighteenth century, the origins of the threshing-machine are lost in obscurity. Credit is usually given for the invention to Andrew Meikle, of East Lothian, who operated a machine, very similar in principle to the modern version, in 1786, but other inventors had been at work before him. Indeed, the first man to hit on the idea of threshing grain by rubbing it between rollers instead of beating it out with flails seems to have been a Mr Ilderton, who lived at Alnwick, Northumberland, around 1774. A good deal of research into the subject was going on in Scotland and the northern counties of England about that time. By the end of the century threshing-machines, mostly driven by horse-power but some by hand, were in fairly wide use in Scotland, though less so in England.

During the next thirty years they spread rapidly and eventually sparked off the farm labourers' last revolt in the autumn of 1830. Horse-gear, driven by a horse which walked in a circle, was the general motive power of the early machines, but from 1848 onwards they began to be powered by steam. Some of the leading manufacturing firms were turning out traction engines by 1853, and by the end of the century these machines, owned by contractors and hauling behind them threshing-machine and elevator, were common-place in the countryside and were tackling most of the thresh-ing. This state of affairs prevailed till the introduction of the combine-harvester.

An integral part of the final threshing-machine was the winnowing apparatus, but its incorporation was a late deve-lopment, and from the earliest times winnowing was a separate operation. The most primitive method, mentioned in the Old Testament, consisted of tossing the grain and chaff into the air and allowing the wind to carry the chaff away. This was the reason why, in countries where fine weather could be relied on, such as Palestine, open-air threshing-floors were generally situated on hill-tops. In England a compromise was reached by throwing the corn the whole length of the barn through a cross-draught caused by opening doors on both sides. Throughout mediaeval times there are references to winnowing fans, which were round and seem to have been made first of wicker and later of canvas. As late as 1796, however, William Marshall, surveying the *Rural Economy of the West of England*, refers to women taking the corn on packhorses to the tops of tors in Devon and Cornwall, there to winnow it by tossing it in the wind. An early and rather slight attempt at mechanization was the sail-fan or 'fan-tackle and chogger'. This was operated by two men, one of whom, by turning a handle, worked a kind of cake-walk from which the grain was shaken out to fall in front of a set of canvas sails, kept in motion by another man turning a handle. My father saw one of these bits of apparatus being used in Wiltshire in the 1880s. Separate winnowing-machines, operating on the same principle but more tidily encased in a box, were in fairly general use by the end of the eighteenth century. I still have one in workable order on my farm. By the 1860s, however, most threshing-machines had winnowing apparatus incorporated in them.

The other main accessory of the threshing-machine, the straw-elevator, was also being linked with it about this time, though those shown at the Royal Show at Worcester in 1863 were considered by the judges to be too cumbersome and expensive. As the designs improved towards the end of the century elevators began to be used for rick-building at harvest and haymaking, as well as for stacking the straw after threshing.

Grain-drying

A whole series of writers in antiquity, beginning with the Greek traveller Pytheas, who visited Britain in 330 B.C., refer to the difficulties experienced by our Celtic ancestors in harvesting and storing corn in a climate which seems to have been no better then than it is nowadays. Says Pytheas, 'they collect the sheaves in great barns and thresh out the corn there, because they have so little sunshine that our open threshing-places would be of little use in that land of cloud and rain'.

The Laws of Howell Da, a mass of details about the lore and customs of the tribes of South Wales compiled in the tenth century, give a good deal of information about agricultural practice which must have applied to the Celtic world for many centuries. From them we learn that kilns for drying grain were part of the standard equipment of the Celtic farm. The kilns were apparently quite large buildings, being sometimes spacious enough for threshing to take place in them. It seems to have been the practice to dry the corn before threshing, the sheaves or loose stalks being spread on racks above a slow fire built on a stone hearth. Sometimes the corn was placed on a large wicker sieve held by hand over heated flints. And sometimes, apparently, the straw was burnt by handfuls and the grain cleverly knocked out while the husks were burning.

The Romans naturally improved on the primitive Celtic kilns, equipping their barns with hypocausts similar to those which heated their bathrooms. Kilns for drying corn are mentioned in both Saxon and Norse literature, and as late as the seventeenth century kilns in which beans and sometimes cereals were dried seem to have been in fairly common use.

Most of the ancient kilns, except the Roman, were designed to dry small quantities of corn at once, and as yields increased they became inadequate for the purpose. It was found, presumably, that grain tied in sheaves and allowed to dry in the field, and afterwards stored in well-made stacks for several months, would keep perfectly well, and for at least two hundred years this method became standard practice. It is only since the introduction of the combine-harvester has presented farmers with the problem of dealing with vast quantities of dampish grain that we have had to learn all over again the art of drying. Nearly all the increasingly numerous devices for the purpose have been evolved since the Second World War, and we are still in the middle of the story.

MILLS

A short account of the storage of grain will be given when we consider farm buildings, but here we must briefly examine the next stage in the treatment of grain, namely, its milling.

The earliest mills were simple, hand-operated querns, common on Iron Age sites and remaining in use until at least Tudor times. Both water-mills and windmills were known in the Roman world, the latter having been introduced in the reign of the first emperor, Augustus. It seems likely that water-mills were operated in Roman Britain, but probably not till slavery was abolished after the triumph of Christianity in the fourth century. Before then most of the milling was done by slaves pushing around, by means of a projecting handle, a large and heavy stone mill. Similar mills for which oxen, donkeys and horses provided the motive power were also in use. Until the coming of the water-mill, grinding corn was almost always a process carried out on the farm.

Water-mills were extensively employed by the Saxons, the Domesday Book being full of references to them. By feudal law everyone in the manor had to have his corn ground by the lord's mill, and hence to pay toll, and a good deal of unrest was caused from time to time by the suppression and destruction of home querns, whereby poor families endeavoured to evade this expense. Horse-powered mills and tidal mills were also known in mediaeval times.

The first reference to a windmill in England is dated 1119 and concerns one erected by a rural dean named Herbert at Bury St Edmunds. Although he was forced by an indignant Abbot to demolish it, by the next century windmills were common.

In mediaeval England the miller was allowed to sell only the grain which he took as his toll and was prohibited, in fact, from becoming a merchant. His stock of poultry was also, for obvious reasons, limited to three hens and a cock! Later he became a true middleman, buying grain from the farmers and selling it to bakers.

Thereafter milling was removed from the farm and so is outside our province. We may mention, however, that small hand-mills for use on the farm, with iron rollers instead of mill-stones, were being manufactured in the 1750s.

The local miller, after having played his part in the rural scene for many centuries, began to find himself dispossessed when the huge influx of foreign grain, beginning in 1875, made essential the establishment of giant mills at ports of entry. The milling business was from that time gradually taken over by big companies who, by research and the development of compound rations, have served the farmer well. During the past twenty years, however, the mill has come back to the farm, more and more farmers installing milling and mixing devices in order to process their home-grown grain for feeding to livestock. Most of these mills are electrically driven.

OTHER BARN MACHINERY

Among the agricultural inventions of the eighteenth century were a number concerned with the cutting of roots and straw. The first chaff-cutter appeared in the 1760s, and for the next hundred years this relatively unimportant aspect of animal feeding attracted far more attention than it was worth. Numerous awards were given by the Royal Agricultural Society of England and by other agricultural societies.

The more important root-cutters came on the scene about the same time, though it was not until the 1830s and 1840s that they were perfected for general farm use. Though still retained in districts where swedes are extensively grown, they have largely disappeared from those parts of the country where their use was chiefly confined to mangolds, now replaced by kale and silage.

Future historians will have to deal with apparatus for chopping and blowing kale and for handling and storing damp grain, but these are innovations so recent as to have, at present, virtually no history.

TOOLS FOR LAND RECLAMATION AND MAINTENANCE

The common tools of maintenance on most English farms were the bill-hook of different types (for hedging) and the spade (for draining and ditching).

The laying and maintenance of the traditional English hedge were too fine an art ever to be satisfactorily mechanized. It has been only very recently, as the overgrown hedges of the neglected years of the depression have been tackled regardless of conventional methods, that power-driven hedge-cutters (most of them working on the principle of the circular or chain saw) have been developed.

The extensive drainage operations undertaken by the Romans in the Fens and elsewhere were carried out by what was virtually slave labour, no doubt employing the most primitive tools. Archaeological evidence shows that early drains and water conduits were frequently made from hollowed tree-trunks.

Seventeenth-century writers (including Walter Blith, 1652, and J. Worlidge, 1668) are the first to mention special implements for draining, their references being to trenching ploughs equipped with long blades to cut an extra deep furrow. In the early eighteenth century the Cambridgeshire draining-plough cut a trench 18 inches wide at the top, 1 foot wide at the bottom and 1 foot deep, and needed twenty horses to pull it. About the same time tile drains began to be used for field drainage, coming into common use about a hundred years later.

The first patent for a mole plough was taken out in 1797,

but somewhat similar ploughs had probably been in use in the eastern counties, notably Essex, for many years previously. A digging-machine was invented by a Norfolk man, Mr Paul, in the 1850s; and in the subsequent decades very heavy tackle, operated by steam power, was produced for cutting trenches, laying pipes and filling in the trenches again.

One of the great advances of the post-war years has been the development of powerful earth-moving machinery. Within the horizons of the general farmer the most important is the bulldozer, now employed extensively in levelling sites, eliminating hedges and in other tasks which formerly would have made prohibitive demands on hand labour. Far heavier machinery is available for semi-industrial use, such as open-cast mining and the subsequent restoration of the land. Excavating machinery, usually operated by contractors, make short work of digging trenches for drainage or the installation of water-pipes; while one of the most useful tools on the farm is the foreloader, hydraulically operated on the front of the tractor.

IRRIGATION

Although the tradition in Wiltshire is that the water-meadows of the chalk valleys were laid out by 'Dutchmen' in the eighteenth century, a hundred years earlier Gabriel Plattes and other writers refer to irrigation as a fairly recent but 'one of the most universal improvements'. This irrigation was of meadow-land and was accomplished by leading water from a stream through a series of interlacing channels, controlled by a system of dams and hatches.

In that age of abounding new ideas schemes were put forward for irrigation by means of the 'Persian wheel', which raised water to a higher level by an endless chain of earthenware pots, and others for raising it by windmills.

The modern system of irrigation by means of pumps forcing water through portable pipelines laid on the surface of fields is entirely new.

TOOLS FOR USE WITH LIVESTOCK

From this section we exclude implements for which animals provide, or provided, the motive power, these having been dealt with elsewhere. We are left with machines employed in dealing with animal products, and we will narrow the field still further by confining it to products yielded while the animal is still alive. In old-time farming the killing and processing of domestic animals was a normal part of farm life. Meat, hides, horn, tallow, bones and feathers were all utilized on the farm which produced them. Nevertheless, by the time the simple home tools of these various crafts were replaced by mechanical methods the work had passed out of the hands of the farmer into those of the butcher, tanner, fertilizer manufacturer and other specialists and are so removed from our province.

The most important agricultural product yielded by living animals nowadays is milk. As we have seen, sheep rather than cows may have been the first animals kept for milk production, cattle being valued primarily for their traction abilities. Milk was a by-product of the animal which pulled the plough and the cart, and most of the small quantities given were made into cheese or butter. Milking and the processing of milk were women's jobs, and even as late as the present century dairy farmers were regarded as an inferior race by the aristocratic sheep and corn and beef farmers (who, incidentally, went bankrupt in the 1920s and early 1930s while their despised teat-pulling neighbours survived).

Attempts at mechanization in the milking-shed did not begin until the second half of the nineteenth century. An American milking-machine was exhibited in 1862, and by 1878 American inventors were working along the right lines, with machines using a vacuum. The Scots and Danes were also early in the field, numerous models being produced by Scottish farmers in the 1880s. Most had serious defects, one of the

39   Pasture irrigation with Wright Farm Sprinkler.

0   A forage-harvester, discharging chopped grass for silage into a
tractor-drawn forage-box.

41 Milking bale, Minchington Farm, Farnham, Cranborne Chase.

42 Modern milking parlour, with Alfa-Laval equipment.

most important being that they worked by continuous suction;
Dr Alexander Shields, of Glasgow, was the first inventor, in
1895, to produce a milking-machine operating on the pulsator
principle. Difficulties were also experienced with the engine
and with keeping the milk clean, but these were gradually
overcome until, by about 1910, fairly efficient machines of
modern types were available.

Cream-separators ante-dated milking-machines by several
decades. They seem to have been first developed on the
Continent, notably in Germany and Scandinavia, and a
German-made model, the Laval, was exhibited at the Royal
Show in 1879.

The inventive years of the late eighteenth and early nineteenth centuries saw the introduction of a variety of machines,
some of them cumbersome and complicated, to aid in butter-
and cheese-making. Even the familiar barrel-churn was apparently not invented until about 1750.

Of recent dairying inventions, probably the most important
was that of the portable milking-bail, developed by Mr A. J.
Hosier on his Wiltshire downlands in the 1930s. This concentrated all the essentials of a dairy into a shed on wheels,
easily moved about the pastures by a tractor, and so enabled
efficient use to be made of grassland far removed from existing
buildings.

The other two agricultural products which concern us here
are wool and eggs.

The first mechanical clippers to supersede the traditional
shears were developed in Australia and were first exhibited in
Britain in 1893. They did not come into fairly general use
until the 1920s.

The first ten or fifteen years after the Second World War
saw a considerable interest in egg-washing machines, most of
them powered by electricity, but this proved ephemeral as the
emphasis shifted to designing poultry houses in which the
eggs would not become dirty.

F.I.B.—N

TRANSPORT

Two-wheeled carts and four-wheeled waggons, the traditional farm transport, were all-purpose until quite recently, when specialized vehicles have been developed.

Carts and sledges were used in Neolithic times and waggons probably in the Bronze Age. In the Glastonbury Lake Village, dating from the first century B.C., four-wheeled vehicles have been found, some with solid wheels and some with spokes. Saxon and mediaeval carts seem often to have had sides of hurdle-work and were probably drawn more frequently by oxen than by horses.

By the sixteenth century different types of carts and 'wains' were recognized, examples being the tumbrel, the corn-wain, the muck-wain and the marling-wain. Experiments were made in the following centuries to mitigate jolting, and regional types of carts and waggons developed. Waggons and carts produced during the past two centuries were often works of art, efficient for their work and beautifully made by skilled craftsmen.

The first reaction of farmers acquiring tractors was to adapt their old farm vehicles for use with the new machines, and many a village blacksmith was called upon to make a towing-bar to replace the shafts on a waggon. It is only since the Second World War that most farmers have invested in tractor-trailers with pneumatic tyres, many of them now with hydraulic tipping gear. Specialized trailers include dung-spreaders and forage-boxes, the latter being now often equipped with an unloading device. Many machines which were formerly drawn first by horses and then by tractors are now self-propelled, and the farm lorry is basically a self-propelled cart.

POWER

We have noted that for thousands of years human and animal muscles were the main sources of power, on farms and elsewhere. The adoption of Christianity by the Emperor Constantine in the fourth century led to the abolition of slavery in the Roman world and hence to an interest in alternative sources of power, resulting, as we have noticed, in some development of water- and windmills. The irruption of the barbarian nations, however, arrested progress for centuries, and some regions relapsed so far into savagery as to forget even the use of the yoke, tying, instead, the plough to the tail of the ox.

No new sources of power appeared till the invention of the steam engine in the eighteenth century. In 1786 the American Thomas Jefferson saw steam engines being used in England to drive mills. Nearly twenty years earlier (in 1767) a farmer, Francis Moore, invented a 'fire engine', of the ability of which to supplant horses he was so convinced that he sold all his own horses and advised his neighbours to do the same, before the slump came! In 1812 the Cornish inventor, Richard Trevithick, was producing steam engines for threshing and grinding corn and for sawing wood. About this time the sugar- and cotton-planters of the West Indies and the southern states of America took up the steam engine and made considerable progress in adapting it for their own purposes.

In England much effort and ingenuity were expended in trying to use steam power for ploughing and other cultivations, the difficulty being that then only stationary engines were available. After several decades of debate and design, a good workable traction engine was produced by Clayton and Shuttleworth in 1859. Thereafter it was a matter of exploring the possibilities for economical use of the steam traction engine on the farm. Because of its size and weight it became most popular on the heavier soils of the eastern counties, where it was made to pull multi-furrow ploughs through stiff clay. Light-land farmers considered, probably erroneously, that it was too heavy to be of much use to them. It achieved, however, universal recognition as a contractor's machine for threshing.

Meanwhile, in America an internal-combustion engine was first harnessed for agricultural use in 1889. An oil-fuelled tractor was exhibited at the Royal Show in 1897, and the age of the tractor really arrived when the Americans began pouring Fordsons into Europe in 1917.

The past twenty years have seen the development of the diesel engine and also the employment of the aeroplane, and more particularly the helicopter, in agriculture, chiefly for spraying and for spreading lime and manure.

ELECTRICITY

Interest in the practical uses of electricity in agriculture began at the end of the First World War, when the British Electrical Development Association started to survey the possibilities. The Government was slow to give financial backing, and consequently rural electrification proceeded piecemeal, partly on the initiative of local authorities and partly by special government schemes, as, for instance, a large one in the west Midlands designed primarily to combat unemployment. Less than 20% of English farms were connected with the grid in 1940, but by 1960 the proportion had risen to 81·5%. The task of connecting all accessible farms will be virtually complete by 1971.

Electricity is the farmyard servant. It provides power for such installations as milking-machines, mills, grain-driers, augers, pumps, hay-driers and cooling and refrigerating plant, as well as for light. In modern poultry-houses electric light is also made to play an important part in stimulating growth and egg production. Electricity is a powerful aid to attaining environmental control by helping to regulate ventilation, humidity and temperature in houses for the mass production of livestock. And new uses are continually being found for it.

One of the most important applications of electricity is to be found in the electric fence, which has made possible the intensive use of grassland and fodder crops by grazing animals. Here the system is independent of the electricity grid, fencing units being run from a portable battery.

8

THE STORY OF OUR
FARM BUILDINGS

IN this very short chapter we shall make a brief survey of an aspect of farming which is assuming increasing importance. Originally farm buildings were intended for shelter, storage and protection from enemies. Lately, as farms tend to be run more and more on factory lines, they are required to give that almost complete control of environment on which economical mass production is based.

In the earliest farmsteads a common hut was doubtless occupied by both humans and animals (or at least by the smaller ones). The larger animals were penned at nights in corrals with earth or stone ramparts, many of the earthworks which crown our hills having originated not as forts but as cattle enclosures.

At the early Iron Age farm at Little Woodbury, in Wiltshire, evolution had taken a further step, for we find there some evidence of partitions, probably for the purpose of allocating certain sectors of indoor space to animal stalls and others for sleeping-quarters. Here also are grain stores. All except the seed corn was stored in subterranean pits (after a preliminary roasting), which had to be abandoned because of bacterial action after five or six years. A great number of these pits, subsequently filled with rubbish, are therefore found not only at Woodbury but at many Iron Age sites. The seed-corn was stored in granaries raised on posts.

From these somewhat primitive farmsteads history takes us straight to the sophisticated Roman establishment. The Roman villa was, in fact, the headquarters of a great agricultural estate and corresponded with the eighteenth- and nineteenth-century country house. In addition to the mansion occupied by the owner, there would be a bailiff's house and quarters for the slaves. Some Roman employers seem to have provided separate bath-houses, of the elaborate Roman sort, for their slaves. Around the courtyard other buildings would contain stalls for oxen and horses, and there would be granaries, storehouses and cellars. Outside the walled court-yard may have clustered a small group of houses inhabited by freedmen, who were, in fact, tenant farmers, paying rent in cash.

The Roman masters of Britain had an eye for the best sites, as their excavated villas illustrate. Elsewhere in the country Celtic tribal life went on as in the old days, though doubtless with more and more of the Roman polish rubbing off on it. Tribal chiefs became Roman country gentlemen, adopting Roman ways, and the lower orders followed suit as far as their economic means would allow them.

In later years, when the decline of the Roman Empire had set in, some of the villas were evidently used as factories, those in the Cotswolds producing cloth.

The Saxon model farm went back to the old Celtic idea of having everything under one roof. We may imagine a thatched, timber building, rectangular in plan, with large entrance doors opening on to a central threshing-floor. Above this floor the corn harvest was stored in a loft and thrown down during the winter for threshing on the floor; hence this compartment of the building was known as the threshold. On one side of it lay the farmer's quarters, consisting, in the simplest form, of a hall with private chambers for the women; also a storehouse. On the other were stalls for oxen and horses, and also a feeding space where their fodder could be spread.

Two other types of farmhouse were coeval in Britain with this Saxon model. In the Celtic west one of the commonest patterns was the booth, in which the framework was provided by pairs of trees, their branches appropriately lopped, which were set in the ground opposite each other to form rude Gothic arches. Such houses could be extended to any desired length by adding more pairs of trees, and space was found inside for all the family's animals and stores. Celtic tribes possessed two sets of houses, one substantially made in the valleys for winter use, and the much lighter summer houses on the hills.

To the regions which they settled the Danes and Norsemen brought their own distinctive architecture. Their houses consisted of great timber halls, the roofs supported by rows of internal pillars, like a church. Little sleeping-chambers were built around the pillars, and a long hearth extended the length of the building. Lofts were also used for sleeping. The Norse houses were inhabited almost exclusively by humans, separate quarters being provided for the domestic animals in adjacent buildings, the whole farmstead being surrounded by a wall. The Norse were among the cleanest nations of antiquity and often chose to build their halls over a stream, thus ensuring a constant supply of running water.

In the Norman manors the livestock were likewise banished to the courtyard. With the house itself we have therefore little concern, but we may remind ourselves that the mediaeval barn was sometimes truly enormous. Surviving tithe barns are magnificent buildings, comparable with some of our finer churches. Mediaeval dovecotes have likewise great artistic merit, and we may be sure that many of the timber houses for cows, sheep, pigs, horses and poultry, of which we read, were well constructed and handsome. The hovels of the lower peasantry, however, were humble affairs of wattle, clay, wood and turf, and doubtless their meagre livestock was similarly poorly housed.

A wholesale rebuilding of rural England occurred, as Dr W. G. Hoskins has recently pointed out, between 1570 and 1640, largely because of the increased prosperity of the yeoman farmer. A typical small farm of this period which I have studied (significantly called 'Model Farm') was built to a ⌐-shaped pattern, the house facing, in accordance with Elizabethan preference, north-east. It was built on flint foundations and was half-timbered and thatched, the spaces between the timbers being mostly filled with plastered wattle-work. One wing consisted of the dairy, wash-house and earth closet; the other of a stable, cattle shed and cart shed. A granary stood separately on staddle-stones in the cobbled yard. Everything was therefore thoughtfully sited around the dwelling-house, so that, as an Elizabethan writer postulates, 'the goodman lieing in his bed may lightlie heare what is doone in each of them with ease, and call quicklie unto his meinie if anie danger should attack him'.

The particular farm I have in mind continued to be served by its Elizabethan farmstead until the 1950s. Others very similar are still in use, as are some more ancient, the great tithe barn at Tisbury, in Wiltshire, for instance, being still filled with corn sacks and farm implements as in its mediaeval prime.

In the great years of agricultural improvement several writers, notably Arthur Young and William Marshall, turned their attention to the ideal plan for the farmyard. They visualized an all-purpose farm, with a concentration of live-stock and stored crops at a centre adjacent to the house. By this arrangement the animals could be fed and littered from stores in the neighbouring barn, while from them in turn such products as milk could be passed to the farm dairy, and from thence the buttermilk and whey could be diverted back to the pigsty. It was all well thought out. One idea with a modern ring was that farm effluent should not be allowed to run to waste, but should be collected for use on the land.

Most sets of farm buildings of the eighteenth and nine-teenth centuries have been influenced by these considerations. Another innovation, dating from about this period, is the frequent use of brick for farm buildings.

The chief specialized buildings before the present century were mills, kilns and granaries. Mills, as we have seen, were driven by either wind or water. Water-mills are built around the water-wheel, turned by a spate of water flowing over a dam. Windmills are of three types – smock mills, tower mills and post mills. Smock mills are octagonal buildings of timber and board. Tower mills are usually of brick, with an independent timber head to which the sails are attached. In post mills the whole mill revolves around a massive centre-post. Few remain in use.

Kilns, originally designed for drying grain, were in later centuries used for drying malt and, nowadays, hops. They were once widespread in England, most farms possessing a kiln, even if it were only a lean-to built against the back of the kitchen fire. Now they are, for the most part, confined to Kent, where the fine oast-houses are a distinctive feature of the landscape.

The main essential of a granary is that it shall be both damp-proof and vermin-proof. Our ancestors solved this problem by building them on raised platforms, the pillars of which were designed to prevent rats and mice climbing them. Ricks likewise were built on platforms of hurdle-work resting on staddle-stones, or mushroom-stones. In the nineteenth century these were sometimes replaced by pillars and frame of cast iron.

Thatching retained some of its importance until the middle of the present century. Thatch began its career as the cheapest and handiest material for the farmer, and long generations of farmers practised their craft on houses, barns, cattle sheds, ricks and even mangold clamps and beehives. Special care was taken, especially after the introduction of threshing-machines, to preserve thatching straw in good condition. The combine-harvester eventually altered it all, and nowadays thatching survives (and indeed flourishes) as a luxury craft, supplying the most expensive type of roof for people who appreciate the picturesque and can afford to pay for it.

During the present century, and more particularly during the past thirty years, several fundamental changes have occurred in our attitude towards farm buildings.

We have tended to decentralize or disperse our buildings. The formerly dominant theory of concentrating everything near the farmhouse, though excellent for a general mixed farm intent mainly on subsistence, resulted in congestion and lack of hygiene. We nowadays try at least to keep the machinery store and the livestock department well away from each other.

The development of the milking-bail, with the aid of first the barbed-wire and then the electric fence, made, in the 1930s, the dairy unit independent of the farmyard. At the same time, large-scale poultry-keeping on the farm became common, and the poultry were housed in portable units away in the fields rather than being confined to the dung-heaps of the farmyard.

Since 1950 increasing specialization has occurred, affecting first the poultry industry. The portable units, novelties of the inter-war years, have been replaced by vast houses designed for tens of thousands of birds. Production of table poultry and of eggs have become entirely separate, but, although the houses are differently equipped, the same efforts are made to bring every factor, including temperature, humidity, ventilation and light, completely under control.

Developments in pig housing were more or less parallel, and now similar techniques are being employed in the production of quick-maturing beef and of veal.

Oddly enough, as the requirements for buildings for specialist purposes become more exacting the farmer tends to veer towards all-purpose, or umbrella, buildings for general use. Buildings which are little more than covered yards can be quickly adapted to a variety of uses, from grain storage to beef fattening, from a silage clamp to an implement shed. Many smaller buildings of this type have been erected since the war with the help of the Ministry of Agriculture's grant towards the cost of silos.

Early in the century brick, tile and thatch were supplanted as the commonest building materials by iron and galvanized sheets. Now these have given place to concrete and asbestos, and lately plastics are beginning to appear on the farm. An innovation in the winter during which this book is being written, 1963–64, is the introduction of plastic sacks for compound fertilizers, which enables them to be stored out of doors all the winter without fear of damage by weather, and will save a vast amount of indoor space. The past decade has also seen tremendous interest in slatted floors – a Norwegian and Icelandic idea – for the winter housing of livestock, particularly cattle.

As we noted when discussing grain-drying, one of the most popular ideas at present is to dry the grain where it is to be stored. This has provided the incentive to produce a number of types of storage bins with perforated floors through which drying air can be pumped. An even more far-reaching development has been that of the sealed storage of undried grain. Barley, with a moisture content of 30% or even more, can be safely stored indefinitely in silos of steel plate reinforced with special glass inside and out. Such a method can be used only for grain which is to be consumed on the farm, for the corn will not keep long after removal and processing, but for this purpose it is perfectly satisfactory. It can save much time at harvest.

9

FARMERS' WARFARE

Diseases of livestock – Diseases of farm crops – Farm pests – Farm weeds

THE farmer's life has always been one of incessant war against pests and diseases. I was going to add the weather, but, of course, the efficient farmer learns in time how to use even the English weather as an ally rather than an enemy. Nevertheless, we must give credit to the weather-forecast service, which gives us at least some clues, in addition to our traditional combination of rheumatism and folk-lore, of what to expect.

DISEASES OF LIVESTOCK

A description, let alone a history, of livestock diseases would require a far larger volume than this, so what follows must be a summary of how the battle has gone.

The situation is fortunately simplified by the fact that until men began to write in detail about agriculture in the sixteenth and seventeenth centuries, almost all animal disease is lumped under the general ominous term, 'murrain'. Cattle, sheep, pigs, horses and even poultry fell victims to 'murrain'. Bees also died off wholesale, as did the human population in recurrent epidemics of 'plague'.

In the sixteenth century we find murrain still occurring, with the heads of dead oxen stuck on poles by stricken farmyards, to warn visitors of the danger. J. Worlidge, in 1688, goes as far as to identify murrain as a swelling in the throat which killed cattle, but that was evidently just the symptom he happened to know. In mediaeval times even piglets eaten by their mothers or succumbing to swine fever were said to have fallen victims to murrain. The favourite treatment, at least in Tudor times, seems to have been to bleed an ox affected with murrain, afterwards giving the animal a dose of herbal mixture in ale.

Old-time writers are rather more explicit about the diseases of sheep. In the thirteenth century 'scab', 'rot', 'the red death', 'pox' and 'the polles' are mentioned. 'Scab', a disease which has only recently been mastered, is presumed to have been introduced into England in the 1270s from the Continent, contemporary opinion associating it with imported Spanish sheep. It may have been partly or largely responsible for heavy losses of sheep in 1283. This, however, was only one outstanding year in the dismal procession of disastrous seasons for the mediaeval stock farmer.

Mediaeval remedies were by no means worthless. Sulphur, tar and mercury, mixed with various homely substances, such as butter and lard, were extensively used, as they have been down to the past few years, when scientists have provided more effective drugs.

Sheep pox seems to have appeared in England about a hundred years later than scab, causing heavy mortality towards the end of the fourteenth century. It has now long been extinct here, as has 'the red death', which apparently was a form of redwater. We are still, however, afflicted by liver fluke, which also caused our mediaeval ancestors much trouble.

Little or nothing is recorded of the ailments of pigs, those semi-feral animals, in mediaeval times.

In the eighteenth century the identification of diseases begins to be more specific, and a formidable catalogue they make. Rinderpest, common on the continent of Europe, made periodic appearances, the worst, in the 1740s and 1750s, causing a major upheaval in English country life. Markets and fairs were closed, the movement of cattle was prohibited by local authorities, and even social events such as 'stage plays, puppet shows and publick Dancings' were cancelled. The

Government adopted a slaughter policy, killing and burying infected animals and paying compensation to one-third of their value. It all sounds curiously modern.

Bloat, husk, staggers, milk fever, contagious abortion, mastitis and blackleg were other diseases which took their toll. Remedies were general rather than specific for each disease, applications of tar ointment and bleeding being the most popular. However, stockmen began to have a glimmering of the measures needed to prevent some of their troubles. The isolation of infected animals was beginning to be practised in the eighteenth century, and some Scottish farmers noted a connection between bloat and the grazing of rich clover leys.

Liver fluke continued to be a major scourge of the sheep flock, as were also scab, sturdy, braxy and foot rot. The old Norfolk sheep passed on their endemic disease of scrapie to the new Suffolks. Remedies were much as before, tar being the favourite, though farmers were experimenting with such materials as tobacco juice and gunpowder, unknown to mediaeval flockmasters, needless to say with little effect.

As the eighteenth century progressed, each decade recording important advances in mechanical invention and livestock breeding, thoughtful observers began to be concerned by the lag in veterinary practice. 'To what purpose', wrote one such observer, W. P. Whyte, 'have our graziers spent hundreds of thousands of pounds in improving our breeds of cattle if a variety of diseases be suffered to ravage them without even a serious attempt to control them?'

Meantime in another field the weapons which would eventually master many of these diseases were being forged. In the seventeenth century the Dutchman Anton van Leeuwenhoek, born in 1632, had with his beloved microscope discovered the world of bacteria. A hundred years later an Italian professor of physiology, Lazaro Spallanzani, exploded the theory of spontaneous generation of such micro-organisms. By the end of the eighteenth century the scientific study of animal diseases was well under way, and a veterinary college had been established in 1791.

Throughout the nineteenth century the number of trained veterinary surgeons steadily increased, replacing the old self-trained cattle doctors and herbalists and ousting the farrier from his traditional role of horse doctor. By the end of the century most farms were within reach of a vet., and the channel existed whereby the discoveries of research scientists could be readily conveyed to the practising farmer.

Thereafter, one by one, the diseases which affect livestock were tackled, though we are, of course, still in the middle of the campaign. The diseases fought back. Foot-and-mouth disease first appeared in Britain in 1839, and contagious pleuro-pneumonia in 1841. An epidemic of rinderpest caused the death of over 233,000 animals in 1865. A bad outbreak of sheep pox occurred in 1847.

Rinderpest was tackled by firm government action within a year of its appearance and completely eradicated by 1871. Pleuro-pneumonia was stamped out by 1900. In 1882 the bacillus of tuberculosis was discovered, leading to the eventual elimination of bovine tuberculosis by a well-conducted campaign in the 1950s. The bacillus of contagious abortion was isolated in 1896, and the foot-and-mouth disease virus in 1898; but both have yet to be conquered. The responsibility of the liver fluke for liver rot in sheep was eventually proved in 1862, and success in treating this ancient scourge now seems in sight. Research into the effects of trace elements, such as magnesium, copper, cobalt and molybdenum, belongs almost entirely to the past thirty years.

DISEASES OF FARM CROPS

We know little of the history of crop diseases. The Romans were familiar with some of the rusts which infect cereals, and 'smut' seems to have been introduced into England in the first half of the sixteenth century. In general, however, crop failure

was due to an 'act of God'. Pagan religions had sundry fes-
tivals at which they besought the gods to protect them from
such a visitation, one being the Roman Rubigalia.

What remedies, if any, were attempted in earlier ages we
cannot say. Among the earliest referred to is the eighteenth-
century practice, recorded by William Marshall, of dressing
seed-corn with arsenic, or with a mixture of salt and lime. A hundred years earlier farmers knew better than to sow infected seed,
though they used it for food, after careful washing and baking.

In the seventeenth century, too, when smut had been
established in England for about a hundred years, farmers
were adopting the sensible precaution of dressing the land
with lime or chalk, as a preventive measure. The Norfolk four-
course rotation was a measure capable of reducing the incidence of disease as well as of maintaining fertility. A
preventive treatment dating from the eighteenth century is
copper sulphate, which was still used for dressing wheat seed
until the 1930s, when I spent many an afternoon mixing
wheat with a solution of blue vitriol on the barn floor.

The war against plant diseases followed much the same
pattern as that against animal diseases. Progress had to await
the success of scientific research, news of which, however, took
longer to filter through to the farmer, owing to there being no
intermediary such as the veterinary surgeon in the field.
Indeed, it needed the establishment of the Agricultural
Executive Committees, the National Agricultural Advisory
Service and the present network of farm institutes and other
educational bodies, as well as a lively trade Press, to facilitate
the full flow of information. Most of these developments have
taken place since 1939.

Farmers now have a number of weapons available.

One of the most widely used is seed disinfection, of which
the copper-sulphate treatment was an early example. This was
partially superseded by dressing with copper-carbonate dust
in 1902 and very largely so by organo-mercury dusts, introduced in 1924.

Spraying is another control method, this being used for insecticides and weed-killers as well as fungicides.

As with animals, the deleterious effects on plants of deficiencies of trace elements in soils have been recognized, and such deficiencies can now be rectified by the application of corrective dressings. The beneficial effects of liming, correctly balanced fertilizers and drainage are now thoroughly appreciated. It is known, for instance, that rusts and mildews thrive on crops to which excessive nitrogen has been applied, that adequate lime can prevent club-root in brassicas, and that various root rots occur only in waterlogged soils.

Yet another line of attack is the starving out of diseases that lurk in the soil by refraining from planting a host crop for the requisite number of years. A rest for about two years will, for example, usually take care of take-all, whereas ten to fifteen years at least are required to rid a field of wart disease.

Since 1931 it has been recognized that seed potatoes grown at high altitudes or in northern districts, where the greenfly cannot live, are comparatively free from virus disease, hence the reliance on seed potatoes from Scotland, Northern Ireland, the Isle of Man and certain other areas.

The plant-breeder is, of course, playing an important part in developing varieties immune to this disease and that.

From time to time we encounter setbacks, particularly in wet seasons, but nothing to compare with the great potato famine of Ireland in 1846 and 1847. Then the entire potato crop, on which the rural population relied almost exclusively, was destroyed by attacks of potato blight (*Phytophthora infestans*), which had first appeared in Europe in 1845. Largely as a result, the population of Ireland was reduced by $1\frac{1}{2}$ million in the decade 1841 to 1851.

FARM PESTS

Here again the story is roughly parallel.

The troubles of farmers in the early agricultural ages were

mainly concerned with predatory animals, such as wolves which attacked their stock and deer which ate their crops. Now we have as our chief enemies insects and parasites. Until recent times, too, farmers were much troubled, through lack of fences and the severity of game protection laws, by domestic and semi-domesticated animals. Throughout the Middle Ages we hear complaints of damage by the lord of the manor's pigeons, by straying pigs, by sheep and by protected deer, while the nineteenth-century tenant was equally powerless against his landlord's hares and pheasants.

Preoccupation with these more visible foes tended to obscure the tinier and deadlier enemies. I have a copy of a book entitled *Farm Insects*, written by John Curtis and published in 1859, which is virtually the first ever to be published on the subject. Government-sponsored research into entomological problems really began only in the present century.

Any account of the history of the war against farm pests is therefore the story of very recent events. It is only since 1939, for instance, that we have got the measure of the wireworm menace. A successful method for treating warble-flies was discovered in the 1920s, and until twenty years ago farmers were lucky if they did not need to sow their turnip crops two or three times, the early efforts being destroyed by the turnip flea-beetle. We now have means of dealing with leather-jackets, the sheep-scab mite, black aphides, slugs, lice, fleas and frit-flies, among many other undesirables; but others, such as the potato-root eelworm, which arrived in this country only in 1913, still defy us, the only control being to starve them out by giving the land a rest from potatoes for a number of years.

Among the larger pests, the rabbit was virtually eliminated by myxomatosis in 1953 and subsequent years, but rats and mice are still with us. Most serious of bird marauders is the wood-pigeon, whose numbers not even the severe winter of 1963 could permanently affect. Nevertheless, farmers are starting to question the wisdom of using against even these nuisances some of the weapons which modern science offers, such as drugs. We are beginning to realize the limitations of our congested islands and to appreciate that we should not lightly exterminate wild life which could never be replaced.

FARM WEEDS

A weed is by definition a plant growing where it is not wanted. A garden marigold could, and sometimes is, reckoned a weed by the farmer, while on the other hand it is quite possible that one day the unpleasant nettle, now regarded as a weed of the first order, may be a useful source of protein. The offence of the weed is that it competes with a cultivated plant, stunting and choking it. Therefore the cultivated plant must be aided by the elimination of the weed.

Although doubtless weeding has been practised from time immemorial, cutting and hand-pulling seem to have been the only control methods until the eighteenth century, except for fallowing. The fallow field occupied a recognized place in mediaeval economy, but whether it was deliberately planned to keep down weeds we cannot know. Certainly it was the custom to stir up the fallow with a plough between haymaking and harvest, a procedure which would have that effect.

Jethro Tull's enthusiasm for his horse-hoe introduced to British agriculture an implement admirably designed for weed control. Tull himself constantly emphasized the need for cultivations between sowing and harvest, though he was more concerned with providing the plants with particles of fine soil than with the suppression of weeds. Nevertheless, the horse-hoe not only kept the root-crops (and on Tull's farm the corn-crops, too) free from weeds but in many instances obviated the necessity for a summer fallow.

As with the campaign against farm pests, the control of weeds by means of chemicals has been largely a development of the past twenty years. Already it has achieved almost alarming success. We have selective weed-killers for dealing with nearly every weed specifically; we have general herbicides which kill all; and for really tough and troublesome species we have chemicals which can be worked into the soil in the fallow period of winter. There are weed-killers to be sprayed on when the crop is growing and weed-killers to be applied before the crop germinates. Rachel Carson's recent book *The Silent Spring* is an overstated but natural reaction to the present popular cult of drenching our soil with selective poisons. Without the aid of chemicals we should be unable to achieve anything like our present crop yields and so would be losers from the start in the race to feed the exploding world population, but new ones are being lavished upon us in such profusion that caution is needed.

Meantime, weeds continue to flourish. Each generation of farmers seems to have a new set of weeds to contend with. When I was a boy in the 1920s and 1930s fat-hen or goose-foot was almost unknown in my part of southern England, whereas now it is one of the most abundant of weeds. Recently, within the past ten years, redshank has made its appearance, and goose-grass has vastly increased. Rosebay willow-herb is much commoner than in pre-war years. On the other hand, only once have I ever seen dodder, that scourge of nineteenth-century farmers. Corn-cockle is now rather rare, and few people know darnel, formerly one of the most formidable farm weeds, even though it finds a place in the New English Bible.

For a full account of the ups and downs of specific agricultural weeds the reader is referred to that masterly volume, *Weeds and Aliens*, by Sir Edward Salisbury.

10

MONEY AND MARKETS

FOR those who like their facts neatly arranged in orderly
sequence, the history of the organization of British agriculture
is disconcertingly complex. To get the present situation into
proper perspective we need now to retrace our steps over
ground already covered.

At the beginning of recorded history we find in this
country a tribal system which must have resembled in many
ways that which prevailed in Ireland five or six hundred years
later or in the Scottish Highlands three hundred years ago.
Almost immediately this system had imposed upon it the
advanced and ruthless Roman organization.

Just how far the Britons had got before the Roman invasion
we cannot say, though it seems that in the south-eastern
corner at least they were well on the way to a modest civilization, with a coinage, the beginnings of an urban population,
and a sufficient surplus of grain to build up a considerable
export trade. In A.D. 43 the Romans arrived with their extremely efficient army, their engineers, tax-collectors and
colonists, and proceeded to lay out the countryside according
to their own rigid and formal ideas. Instead of meandering
tracks, roads as straight as a ruler could draw them transected
the realm. In the new towns the streets met each other at exact
right angles, and the holdings for colonists, in numbered
blocks of equal size, were also strictly rectangular. Outside
these alien settlements, the pattern of rural life which evolved
was very similar to that of Victorian England. The country
was divided among great estates, owned either by immigrant
gentry from other parts of the Roman world or by the now-
Romanized Celtic aristocracy. Interspersed were tenant farms
and the surviving settlements of the pre-Occupation Celtic
peasantry, now doubtless heavily taxed. It is true that the

Roman system was based on slavery, but whether the slaves were much worse off than the agricultural labourers of the first half of the nineteenth century is a moot point.

A large volume of trade flowed between Britain and the other provinces of the Roman Empire. As well as grain, metals, notably lead, copper, tin, silver and gold, minerals such as salt, and assorted commodities, including woollen cloth, pottery, jet and Purbeck marble, were exported and many luxuries from the Mediterranean world brought in. Commercial companies existed to exploit the mines, money was in universal use, and the system was almost entirely capitalist.

As we have seen earlier, this highly organized economy foundered almost completely in the unrecorded centuries. The Saxon system, when it emerged was subsistence farming again. Each little community was more or less self-sufficient; the country was divided among small independent states frequently at war with each other; and trade was at a low ebb. Recent evidence suggests that this may not be the complete picture. By the tenth century at the latest the sheep population had grown to such dimensions that there must have been a considerable trade in wool, and there was a good deal of cross-Channel commerce in the reigns of the later Saxon kings.

Nevertheless, the rural Saxon economy, with its thanes and ceorls, was very similar to the Norman one soon to be imposed upon it, with its lords and villeins. This feudal system was based on the idea of service given rather than money paid. The original theory was that, in the lawless days in Europe after the break-up of the Roman Empire, the peasant and artisan should devote part of their time and labour to providing for a class of professional soldiers who would protect them from outside enemies. It developed into the inevitable protection racket, on the best gangster pattern, with eventually an hereditary military aristocracy lording it over a servile population.

Only slowly did the liberating influence of trade penetrate

the self-contained and isolated communities which resulted. Mediaeval towns were small, and trade at first lay chiefly in the hands of foreigners, notably Italians, Flemings, and Jews. We have already surveyed the part played by the wool trade in the growth of English commerce and noted how throughout the Middle Ages the increasing number of royal charters for markets and fairs granted to growing towns and large villages testified to the development of an interest in affairs outside the manor boundaries. The Black Death, as we remarked on page 28, resulted in such a demand for the services of the surviving population that the feudal system could not cope. Labourers, escaping from their hereditary manors, offered their services for wages to the highest bidder. Landowners, despairing of exacting sufficient labour dues to keep their lands in cultivation, let off their farms for money rents. The countryside was well on the road of transition from a feudal to a capitalist system.

The implications of the change were of fundamental importance to the farmer. Instead of being able to fulfil his obligations by giving his time and labour or by handing over part of his produce, he had to find some cash: cash to pay the rent and, if he were farming on a big enough scale, cash to pay the wages. On small farms in areas of low rentals the cash requirements may have been modest enough to allow the farmer to carry on much as before, but elsewhere both incentives and opportunities developed. The obvious place in which to trade farm products for cash was the local market; hence the steady growth of a network of market towns throughout the country. Each thriving little town drew its supplies from the farms of the surrounding villages – as, indeed, still happens to a certain extent and with certain commodities, such as fruit, vegetables, eggs and poultry.

An exception was, however, soon provided by the metropolis. As the centuries rolled past, London became far too large to derive all its supplies from the adjacent fields of Middlesex, Essex, Surrey, and Kent. It drew them from farther and farther afield, until in the seventeenth and eighteenth centuries enormous numbers of cattle and sheep were walking to London, by well-established drovers' routes, from the farthest corners of the kingdom, notably from Wales. Immense flocks of geese and turkeys, too, walked in from the farms of Norfolk and Suffolk. The drovers who controlled this traffic also acted as middlemen for all manner of trade and played an important part in the rural economy.

In time other cities than London grew beyond the capacity of their local farms to feed, a process drastically accelerated by the Industrial Revolution with its seething new towns. The nation was just beginning to adapt itself to the new requirements when the prolonged strain of the war against Napoleon upset orderly progress.

During this war, with its blockade and counter-blockade, food became so scarce that the price of wheat rose from 43s. a quarter before hostilities to 126s. a quarter in 1812. When the war ended prices collapsed suddenly, and to restore some measure of agricultural prosperity a Corn Law, aimed at keeping corn prices at a fairly high level, was passed in 1815. The result was much distress and misery and the growth of a feeling of antagonism between town and country.

The Corn Laws were repealed in 1846. By this time the country had settled down after the marathon efforts of the wars with the French, and 1850 to 1875 was a period of agricultural prosperity. Then, as we have seen, grain, and later meat and dairy products, started pouring in from the newer countries of the world.

The consequent plight of agriculture was regarded without sympathy by the urban population, which now controlled British policies. After their early Victorian experience of protective legislation, as exemplified by the Corn Laws, the voters of the second half of the century were overwhelmingly in favour of Free Trade. And this was to a degree logical, for Britain, the greatest manufacturing nation in the world and

head of a vast maritime empire, lived by selling its manufactured goods to countries which could pay only in primary
products, such as food. The perils of abandoning such a
fundamental industry as agriculture were not yet realized.

The nation received its first major lesson in this department
during the 1914–18 War, when the Kaiser's U-boats were able
to threaten it with starvation. But the lesson was soon forgotten when the danger had passed, and from the early 1920s
to about 1938 farming struggled in one of the worst depressions it had ever known.

From the hardships of the first forty years of the twentieth
century emerged two events pregnant with the promise of
better things for agriculture. One was the formation of the
National Farmers' Union in 1908; the other the establishment
of the Milk Marketing Board in 1933. The latter was an
experiment in an entirely new principle, the marketing of a
farm commodity on a national basis by a producer-controlled
organization. Operating a monopoly in the sale of milk, it
pooled the receipts and allocated them to producers in price
ranges which took account of geography, the calendar and, to
some extent, quality. Though severely criticized at the beginning, particularly by farmers who saw large quantities of
'surplus' milk being sold for manufacture at give-away prices,
the Milk Marketing Board succeeded in proving its value and
has served as a pattern for other similar organizations. In
recent years it has, by a clever advertising campaign, boosted
the sales of 'liquid' milk to a level far surpassing that in
most other countries, besides exercising a strong influence in
matters concerning the breeding of dairy cattle.

The beginning of the 1939–45 War found British agriculture in a semi-moribund condition. More than 70% of the
country's food was imported. Millions of acres of land lay
derelict or was growing only the roughest of grass, much of it
changing hands at a few pounds per acre. Many farms were
let rent-free for years, simply in order to obtain a tenant.
From extensive areas sheep, on which the farm economy had

F.I.B.–P

traditionally been based, had disappeared. Buildings were un-repaired and often ruinous, few farms had adequate mechan-ical equipment, and the industry had been drained of capital.

To enable this run-down agriculture to face its new and urgent challenge the Government appointed in each county and each district War Agricultural Executive Committees. These consisted of prominent and progressive farmers, with the Ministry of Agriculture's technical staff to provide administration and give guidance and advice. It was their duty, by stick-and-carrot methods, to ensure that maximum production was achieved. A ploughing-up campaign for old grassland was initiated; new agricultural machinery shipped in from America under Lend-Lease agreements was allocated; and the principles of good husbandry were encouraged and, where necessary, enforced. Agriculture fulfilled its wartime task with great credit, and with the end of hostilities seemed poised for a new era of prosperity.

Cynical old-time farmers, who had seen much the same sequence of events in and after the 1914–18 War, prophesied a speedy relapse to the old pattern of neglect and depression, but this time they were wrong. Doubtless the continuance of the 'Cold War', with Russia instead of Germany as the rival, was a potent factor in determining the country's policies. In 1947 the passing of the Agriculture Act gave agriculture a stable background which has been maintained ever since. Chief elements are a system of guaranteed prices based on an annual price review and if necessary supported by govern-ment subsidies.

The State's involvement in agricultural prices during the past one hundred and fifty years may be summarized as follows: *Laissez faire* during the Napoleonic Wars, to the detriment of the consumer; price-fixing from 1815 to 1846, maintaining prices at an artificially high level for the benefit of the producer and to the detriment of the consumer; *laissez faire* from 1846 to 1939, with beneficent consequences to everyone till 1875 and after that disaster to the producer; price control from 1939 to the present day. During this last period price control operated to the benefit of the consumer while the war lasted, prices being kept artificially low. Since then its effect has been controversial. Abandonment of the machinery for giving farmers guaranteed prices would result, it is now generally agreed, in the cost of most agricultural goods rising to consumers, but arguments on the desirability of this continue to rage.

The success on the Continent of the European Economic Community caused, in the early 1960s, the Government to reconsider the pros and cons of joining that organization. The professed aim of the Community is to organize its constituent members (France, West Germany, Italy, Belgium, the Netherlands, and Luxembourg) into an economic entity, with trade barriers eliminated because of the establishment of a system of common prices and costs, including wages. As the internal barriers went down so the external ones seemed likely to go up, to keep out all but the products which could not be produced economically or in sufficient quantity inside the Community – a consideration which caused the British Government to decide that the country would be better off inside than out. Negotiations to this end were far advanced at the beginning of 1963 when General de Gaulle, the French President, called a halt by imposing impossible conditions. The scheme is, however, probably only in abeyance. In due course we are likely to find ourselves involved with our Continental neighbours in an association which will approach, if it does not actually become, complete integration. The ultimate effects on British agriculture can as yet only be guessed at.

Meantime, the internal organization of home farming is changing rapidly. The farmers who survived the Great Depression were those who could cut their spending to a minimum. This state of affairs set a premium on the peasant-type subsistence farmer, who employed no one outside his own family and met each crisis by reducing his standard of living. By an arrangement which saved the Inland Revenue

Department a lot of fruitless trouble, the farmer's income in the bad days of the 1930s was reckoned to be the equivalent of his rent. As this kept him well below the level at which he would have to pay income tax, he was also saved the trouble of keeping account books. Few farmers in those days practised any sort of book-keeping other than the ledger accounts in which they recorded debts owed and owing.

With the changes in taxation during the 1939–45 War, farmers were forced into adopting more businesslike methods. Moreover, these new methods and the new machines they needed continually increased the amount of capital they had to invest. This proved one of the major handicaps for an industry emerging from so long a period of depression, but the problem has gradually been solved.

A measure of the investment of capital in agriculture is provided by the figures of advances made to farmers by British banks. In 1946 the total was £70,880,000; in 1963 it was £410,612,000. This is matched by the probable increase in the investment of the farmers themselves, and is augmented by a vast amount of merchant credit. One reason for the credit-worthiness of farmers lies in the galloping rate of increase in the value of land. Much land bought in the 1930s for £5 and £10 an acre is now worth £200 to £300 an acre even for agricultural purposes, and far more for building or other development. The apparent wealth of many old-established farmers is based not so much on their farming activities as on this prodigious appreciation of capital invested in land. Nevertheless, the result is a sound and now well-capitalized agriculture, able to make the heavy investments in modern equipment now demanded of it.

Now that big money is involved, big business is beginning to creep in. The second half of the nineteenth century saw the growth of the limited liability company in urban industry; now it is invading agriculture. Not only are many large farms now run as private limited liability companies, but commercial empires are being formed to control certain spheres of production. The poultry industry has been one of the first thus to be taken over. During the past ten years by far the greater part of the table poultry and egg production of this country has passed into the hands of a few giant firms. Now the process is starting with meat and other commodities.

One incentive is the growth of a new type of market. The latter years of the nineteenth century saw the auctioneer being interposed between the farmer and purchaser at markets and fairs. Now, except for store stock, the markets themselves are being superseded by direct contracts negotiated between farmers and manufacturers. Under this system farmers have the advantage of producing for a known market and at known prices, which greatly aids budgeting and planning. As the demand grows, however, for very large quantities of a standard product, so farmers are being forced to realize the need for an organization on their side equal to that of the buyers on the other. The stage is set for the growth of larger and larger farming units and for the development of more powerful marketing organizations.

In the former connection, one of the features of post-war farming has been the growth of the agricultural estate. Before the war most owners of agricultural estates let much of their land to tenant farmers, apart from a home farm retained to supply the needs of the family. Now most are farming their estates on a sound commercial basis, enlarging their units by taking in hand any tenanted farms which become vacant.

Another method whereby the size of agricultural holdings is being increased is by the amalgamation of farms, often by the purchase of adjacent units by prosperous farmers, but sometimes through the deliberate intervention of landlords.

Yet another is the slower and more difficult one of co-operation. During the 1950s there came into being an organization called Credit Syndicates Ltd, sponsored by the National Farmers' Union and formed for the purpose of enabling groups of farmers to acquire expensive machinery on favourable credit terms. Many groups of farmers who, through forming machinery credit syndicates, have had experience of the advantages of co-operation are now experimenting with more advanced schemes, the eventual effect of which may be to build up units of interlocking though independent farms integrated both as to production and distribution.

11

THE FUTURE?

WHETHER the historian has any business to try to look into the future is a debatable proposition.

As far as the technical aspects of agriculture are concerned, to attempt to do so would be a thankless task. Progress is so rapid that one can simply not foresee what will happen next. Who, for instance, could have forecast, back in the 1940s, the place that the forage-harvester would play in grassland farming? Who can assess at the moment the potential development of the sealed store for wet grain?

We may hazard one or two guesses.

One of the main difficulties of cultivation in this mechanized age lies in the fact that, unless the soil is in good friable condition, the passage of heavy wheeled traffic damages it. Recently there has been demonstrated a vehicle which, by using a cushion of air on the principle of the hovercraft, may be able to overcome this handicap. A radio-controlled flying tank, for distributing a chemical spray or a fertilizer over a crop too tall for the passage of a tractor is also a desirable possibility.

The vast quantities of home-grown barley now milled, mixed and fed on the farms have to be supplemented by concentrated mixtures to balance the rations for protein and minerals. The protein part is supplied largely by imported material, chiefly fish meal, and is expensive. The technique of extracting protein from green matter has been successfully tackled in the laboratory and, with slightly less though still considerable success, on a commercial scale. Leaf protein extraction may well become a farm operation of the future, with crops such as clover leys, lucerne and even nettles grown specifically for processing.

In the livestock world the emphasis is likely to be on

synthetic crosses and hybrids (in all except the breeding of dairy cattle), planned in due course by teams of geneticists, as with poultry at present. This does not mean, however, the eclipse of our pure-bred stock, but rather of an era of prosperity for them, for they must be maintained as a reservoir of the best material from which the scientists can draw supplies.

There are rumours of scientific advances which will enable us to determine the sex of animals at will, but the implications of this and of the technique, now being perfected, of transplanting fertilized ova into host mothers we must wait for the future to reveal.

As we have seen, the politics and economics of farming are likely to become bound more closely with those of the European Economic Community (*alias* the Common Market). The changes which would be triggered off by our entry into the Community would be so revolutionary that to try to crystalgaze would be a waste of time at the moment.

Nevertheless, we can say that there is no sign at all of an agricultural recession. Although during the past decade farming has lagged behind much of the rest of the country in income increases, with some resultant hardship, yet basically it remains reasonably prosperous, and its prosperity is likely to increase.

This presumption is based on the fact of there being two commodities the demand for which is rising far in excess of supply, namely, land and food.

It has been calculated that if every interested party, private or public, were to be allowed to use as much land as it declares is absolutely essential, we would have allocated, before the end of the century, more than twice as much land as we have available in the whole of Britain! Clearly, then, the pressure on land is bound to increase, and a more and more intensive use will have to be made of whatever is retained for agriculture.

As for food, with two-thirds of the world already existing on an inadequate diet, we face a population explosion which will increase the total number of the human race to nearly 4,000 million by A.D. 2000.

So far in western Europe we have been in a favourable position. We have enjoyed far more than our share of the world's food supply. As the emergent nations of the world become more prosperous, however, we shall find them competing strongly in the markets for what there is going. The fact that there is not enough to go round will be reflected in rising prices for us. For it must be remembered that we still import more than half our food.

The task of British farmers, as the century draws to its close, will be the increasingly urgent one of producing more and more from a diminishing number of home acres. The situation may eventually become desperate enough for maximum production to become imperative, almost regardless of cost.

BIBLIOGRAPHY

HISTORICAL

Ashby, M. K., *Joseph Ashby of Tysoe 1859–1919*, Cambridge 1961

Blith, Walter, *The English Improver Improved*, 1652

Clark, Grahame, *Prehistoric England*, Batsford 1940

Cobbett, William, *Cottage Economy*, 1821
Rural Rides, 1821–32

Coleman, Olive, *The Brokage Book of Southampton 1400–1500*, Southampton 1960
The Brokage Book of Southampton 1443–44, (Vol. II), Southampton 1961

Davis, Thomas, *General View of the Agriculture of Wiltshire*, 1811

Denton, W., *England in the Fifteenth Century*

Ernle, Lord, *English Farming Past and Present*, Longmans, Green 1936
(E. Prothero) *Shakespeare's England*, Section xii 'Agriculture and Gardening'

Fleure, H. J., *A Natural History of Man in Britain*, Collins 1951

Fox-Pitt-Rivers, A. H. L., *Excavations at Cranbourne Chase*

Fussell, G. E., *The Farmer's Tools 1500–1900*, Andrew Melrose 1952
Old English Farming Books from 1523–1730, Crosby Lockwood 1947
More Old English Farming Books from 1731–1793, Crosby Lockwood 1950

Hammond, J. L. and Barbara, *The Village Labourer*, (Vols. I and II), Guild Books 1911

Hudson, W. H., *A Shepherd's Life*, Methuen 1910

Lawrence, John, *A General Treatise on Cattle*, C. Whittingham 1764

Marshall, William, *Rural Economy of Yorkshire*, 1787
  Rural Economy of Norfolk, 1787
  Rural Economy of Gloucester, 1788–9
  Rural Economy of the Midlands, 1789
  Rural Economy of the West of England,
1791–96
  Rural Economy of the Southern Counties,
1797
Mascall, Leonard, *Husbandrye Ordring of Poultrie*, 1581
  Countreyman's Jewel or the Government of Cattell, 1591
Markham, Gervase, *Farewell to Husbandry*, 1620
Orwin, C. S., *A History of English Farming*, Nelson 1949
Quennell, Marjorie and C. H. B., *Everyday Life* – series: *Prehistoric Times; Old Stone Age; New Stone, Bronze and Early Iron Ages; Roman Britain; Saxon, Viking and Norman Times*. Batsford, 1924, etc.
Richmond, I. A., *Roman Britain*, Penguin 1955
Ruddock, *Italian Merchants and Shipping in Southampton 1270–1600*, Southampton 1951
Seebohm, M. E., *The Evolution of the English Farm*, Allen and Unwin 1927, revised 1952
Stamp, L. Dudley, *Man and the Land*, Collins 1955
Stanford, J. K., *British Friesians – a History of the Breed*, Max Parrish 1956
Stenton, D. M., *English Society in the Early Middle Ages*, Pelican 1951
Sumner, H., *Ancient Earthworks of Cranbourne Chase*, 1913
Topsell, Edward, *Historie of Foure-Footed Beastes*, 1607
Trevelyan, G. M., *English Social History* (Illustrated), Pelican 1964
  History of England, Longmans 1926, etc.
Trow-Smith, Robert, *A History of British Livestock Husbandry to 1700*, Routledge 1957
  A History of British Livestock Husbandry 1700–1900, Routledge 1959

Tull, Jethro, *The New Horse-hoeing Husbandry*, 1731
Tusser, Thos., *Five Hundred Points of Good Husbandry*, 1573
Wright, Philip, *Old Farm Implements*, A. & C. Black 1961
Young, Arthur, *Northern Tour*, 1770
                 Eastern Tour, 1771
                 Six Weeks' Tour of the Southern Counties, 1772
                 Farmer's Calendar, 1804

GENERAL

Beaven, E. S., *Barley*, Duckworth 1947
Boston, Eric J., *Jersey Cattle*, Faber 1954
Boyd, A. W., *A Country Parish*, Collins 1951
Carson, Rachel L., *The Sea Around Us*, Staples 1951
Darling, F. Fraser, *Natural History in the Highlands and Islands*, Collins 1947
Edlin, H. L., *Trees, Woods and Man*, Collins 1956
Filter, R. S. R., *London's Natural History*, Collins 1945
Fraser, Allan, *Sheep Husbandry*, Crosby Lockwood 1961
Harvey, L. A. and D. St Leger-Gordon, *Dartmoor*, Collins 1953
Hoskins, W. G., *Provincial England*, Macmillan 1963
Jermyn, L. A. S., *The Singing Farmer*, 1947
Journals of the Royal Agricultural Society of England
Nicholson, E. M., *Birds and Men*, Collins 1951
Robinson, D. H., *The New Farming*, Faber 1948
Russell, Sir E. John, *The World of the Soil*, Collins 1957
Stamp, L. Dudley and Hoskins, W. G., *The Common Lands of England and Wales*, Collins 1963
Trow-Smith, Robert, *English Husbandry*, Faber 1951
Vesey-Fitzgerald, Brian, *The Book of the Horse*, Nicholson & Watson 1946

INDEX

F.I.B.—Q

Power, 192–4; electricity, 194; internal-combustion engine, 193–4; steam, 193; steam traction engines, 193
'Pox', sheep, 203, 205
Practical Farmer, The, 82
Pratt, Major, invents cultivating implement, 173
Prehistory of European Society, The, 60–61
Prentice, Thomas, and Scottish potatoes, 87
Price controls, 216–17
Prices, guaranteed, 53–54, 55, 216–17; State involvement in, 216–17
Prongs, early, 18
Provincial England, 127
Pytheas on harvesting and storing grain, 184–5

Quartley, Francis, and Devon Cattle, 118
Querns, 18

Rabbits, 161–2; Angora, 162; Belgian Hare, 162; Beverans, 162; Chinchilla, 162; domestic, 162; Flemish Giant, 162; Havana, 162; mass production of, 162; warrens, 162; wild, 161, 208
Rags as manure, 69
Raleigh, Sir Walter, introduces potatoes, 86
Ransome, Robert, patent for tempering cast-iron shares, 170
Rape, 99–100
Rats, 208; brown, 164

Raynham, 68
Reap-hooks, 177; early, 18
Reapers (reaping), 177–9; mechanical, 177–9
Red Clover, 92, 93, 97; first mention of, 67; in Roman times, 93
'Red death', sheep, 203
Redshank, 210
Reynolds, Mr, introduces kohlrabi, 99
Ribwort plantain, 93
Richmond, Dr I. A., on the Fens, 26
Ricks, 199
Rinderpest, 203–4; 1841 epidemic, 205; eradication of, 205
Rollers, 172–3
Roman Britain (Richmond), 26
Rome, Treaty of, 54
Romney Marsh, sheep on, 128
Root-cutters, 187
Rosebay Willow-herb, 210
'Rot', sheep, 203
Rotary tillage, 173
Royal Jersey Agricultural Society, 123
Royal Show (1851), Large White pigs at, 149
Royal Society report on potatoes (1662), 86
Rural Economy of the West of England, 184
Rye, 77, 85–6; in mediaeval times, 65; Lovaszpatonai, 86; origin of, 17
Rye-grass, 85, 92, 97; as seed-producing plant, 94–5; perennial, 93, 94; S24, 85